CW01635781

HOW TO IMPROVE AND PROTECT YOUR MENTAL HEALTH

Happier Self Worth
Connected Resilient

Eddie Bannon

Ballyholme Publishing

ISBN: 9781739196400 eBook
ISBN: 9781739196417 Paperback

CONTENTS

INTRODUCTION

"You can't stop the waves, but you can learn to swim."

– JON KABAT-ZINN

I am standing at the window of the most famous police station in the world, looking across the River Thames to the London Eye. I have just finished delivering a suicide prevention training programme for police officers and staff. I am gathering my thoughts and equipment before heading to the underground, the airport and then home.

A police inspector approaches and thanks me for the training. She tells me that she liked my approach: straightforward, evidence-based, easy to understand,

and with a model to use in real life. Because of this approach, she wants to ask for some advice. She wants to learn how to protect her mental health as she protects her physical health. She exercises almost every day, enjoys a healthy balanced diet, drinks alcohol moderately, goes to the dentist every six months, and tries to get a good night's sleep as often as her job allows.

She has access to substantial evidence-based information on how to protect her physical health. It is simple to convert this information into actions; if she is worried about something specific, she can talk to her doctor. Unfortunately, she feels it is different regarding her mental health. Information and guidance about mental health aren't as available or as easy to understand, often focusing on recovery from illness rather than avoiding becoming ill in the first place.

Unsurprisingly her job causes her stress, as does her home life for different reasons. As stress is a part of her life that can't be eliminated, she wants to know how to protect herself from its negative impact. Similarly, what can she do about feelings of depression, anxiety, and trauma that affect her from time to time? She doesn't believe she is ill; it is just part of her everyday life, no different from other family members, friends, and colleagues. But she wants to feel better emotionally consistently and is prepared to invest as much time and energy in her mental health as she does in her physical health.

She wants to learn how to do two things. Firstly, what steps can she take to reduce the risk of becoming ill from depression or anxiety? This has happened to too many people in her life. Secondly, how can she feel better on an ordinary day when nothing particularly good or bad happens? Can I recommend a book that will explain how she can thrive emotionally? I am able to give her guidance, pointing to a book on mindfulness, a TED Talk on gratitude, and an article on neuroplasticity. Still, I can't refer her to one book that will give her a comprehensive, evidence-based overview of how to improve her mental health. That conversation led to this book. This is the book I would have loved to have been able to hand her that afternoon.

My hope in writing this book is that it will help you improve and protect your mental health. There is substantial research evidence that you can do so by effecting four important changes in your life. The first change is to increase how often you feel happy and we explain how to do this in chapters 2, 3 and 4. The second change is to develop healthier feelings of self worth, we discuss how to achieve this in chapters 5 and 6. The third change is to build strong connections to the important people in your life, we explore how in chapters 7 and 8. And the final change is to become more resilient and we explain how to achieve this in chapter 9.

Over the years, to develop evidence-based mental health training programmes, I have read thousands of pages of research and watched hundreds of hours of lectures about the causes and treatment of mental disorders. I have recalled my experiences as the director of a suicide intervention charity and the stories of mental health journeys kindly shared by the thousands of participants who have attended my programmes. I have incorporated what I have been privileged to learn and experience into the development of this book, but nothing is included unless it is supported by research-based evidence.

Our knowledge of mental health is constantly changing, but there are clear, widely accepted core skills and habits, validated by evidence, that you can bring into your life to improve and protect your mental health. Just like learning to swim, the time to invest in your mental health is now, not when you find yourself in difficulties. Start introducing them into your life. Today. If you do so, your journey to improve and protect your mental health will have begun.

CHAPTER 1: UNDERSTANDING MENTAL HEALTH

"When I was five years old, my mother told me that happiness was the key to life. When I went to school, they asked me what I wanted to be when I grew up. I wrote down 'happy'. They told me I didn't understand the assignment, and I told them they didn't understand life."

— JOHN LENNON

As the police inspector I talked about in the introduction instinctively understood, mental health is not simply the absence of mental illness or emotional distress. If you could remove all the issues in your life that were making you feel depressed, stressed, anxious, angry or sad, you might expect to feel great. You might assume you would flourish; your days would contain pleasure, joy, contentment, and happiness. Sadly, for most people, that is not the case. Often people recover from depression or anxiety and just feel neutral. The distressing, negative feelings have reduced, but feelings of happiness and joy have not replaced them. This is because moving away from sadness and depression is a separate, though overlapping, process from moving towards happiness and mental health.[1]

Mental health is being happy far more often than being distressed. It is believing you are a human being of worth and not someone burdened with shame. It is feeling deeply connected to the important people in your life. It is recovering after emotional distress or as Maya Angelou said, "You may not control all the events that happen to you, but you can decide not to be reduced by them".[2] And when you are mentally healthy, when you have 'flourishing mental health', you are at a significantly reduced risk of developing depression, anxiety, or other psychological illnesses.[3] You will benefit from investing in your mental health, just as you benefit from investing in your physical health. It will change you, and the life you lead, for the better. You will become more optimistic about the future and appreciative of the past. You will have more positive and diverse relationships in your life. You are likely to earn more money and get promoted more often. You will suffer less mental illness and are likely to outlive your contemporaries. You will become a kinder person with more empathy for your family, friends, and colleagues. You will better appreciate the good things in your life whilst becoming more generous to other people. You will become more forgiving of those who have hurt you, including yourself. Investing in your mental health will be one of the most rewarding things you will do in your lifetime; for your well-being and the well-being of those closest and most important to you.

Improving Your Mental Health Protects You From Mental Illnesses

Investing in your mental health provides substantial protection against the development of common mental illnesses, including clinical depression and anxiety. Researchers studied over a thousand new doctors during their internship year in sixteen medical institutions in the United States.[4] The first year of practice in a hospital is notoriously stressful and often leads to depression. The researchers compared each new doctor's level of mental health before starting their internship year and found that levels of mental health accurately predicted future levels of depression. For almost all these new doctors, their depressive symptoms increased significantly during the year of their internship. The study found that the level of growth in depressive symptoms was significantly linked to their mental health at the start of the year. The higher the levels of mental health at the beginning of the year, the lower the depressive symptoms throughout the year.

People who don't actively invest in their mental health often have what leading research psychologist Corey Keyes calls 'languishing' mental health. They aren't ill, but they aren't that healthy, either. If this describes you, you are up to six times more likely to become clinically depressed than if you are mentally healthy, what he describes as flourishing mental health.[5] Incorporate the skills and habits of mentally healthy people described in this book and you will significantly reduce the chance of developing depression, anxiety, and other common mental disorders.

Improving Your Mental Health Protects Your Physical Health

Actions we take to achieve mental health also reduce the risk of developing physical illnesses, and even the risk of death. A study measured optimism, a material component of mental health, in over 70,000 nurses. The researchers divided the nurses into four groups, the most optimistic through to the least optimistic.

Over six years, they compared the most optimistic group against the least optimistic group for major health outcomes. If you were in the most optimistic group of nurses, you had an almost 30 per cent lower chance of dying of any cause during those six years than if you were in the most pessimistic group.[6]

However, it would be a mistake to believe that investing in your mental health is an alternative treatment for a serious physical illness. Fewer optimistic nurses died because they saw the value in early diagnosis, engaged more often in treatment, and invested in their emotional and physical well-being, including safer diets and more physical activity.

But it is also clear that psychological illnesses such as depression inhibit your body's ability to survive a serious physical illness such as cancer. A cancer diagnosis often triggers overwhelming feelings of depression and anxiety, which sadly further reduces the chance of a positive outcome. A study of over 20,000 patients with cancer found that those with clinical depression were over 40 per cent less likely to survive than patients without depression.[7]

Determining How Mentally Healthy You Are

You know that looking after your mental health is essential, but what does this mean in practice? Three elements determine how mentally healthy you are:[8]

- ***The first element is genetics, which is something you cannot influence.*** Your genes contribute to whether you experience better or worse mental health than your next-door neighbour. However, if you had an identical twin, your mental health could be substantially better or worse than theirs because of your life choices and the investment you make in your mental health.

- ***The second element is the impact of your life circumstances and experiences.*** It will affect your feelings if you have recently been bereaved, been in a car accident, had money troubles, or lost your job. Your mental health, particularly your emotional resilience, will help to determine how badly negative events in your life impact you.

- ***The third element is intentional activity.*** You can choose to undertake actions with the realistic, evidence-based expectation that the result will be improved mental health. This book focuses on intentional activity because it is within your control.

The Four Drivers Of Mental Health

Actions have value when they produce the change you need. This book focuses on activities that research has found will improve and protect your mental health.

Driver 1: Increase How Often You Feel Happy

If you got up this morning, went about your typical day, and had one positive emotion for every negative emotion, how do you think you would feel? You might expect that you would feel ok or neutral. In reality, you would feel depressed, probably very depressed. Why is that? The first element is that our subconscious scans for threats far more than opportunities. If you are out for a walk and find yourself suddenly facing a bear and a cow, you will focus on the bear because it's a threat to your existence. To survive, your brain knows that the danger from the bear is the only thing of importance.

The second element of this negative bias is that we have a massively stronger emotional reaction to a threat than an opportunity. When you spot the bear, a part of your brain called the amygdala triggers your stress response. Your body produces the stress hormone cortisol and adrenaline, which are pumped into your bloodstream. This causes you to take immediate, emotionally driven action to race away from the danger or to attack its source. This is your stress response or flight or fight response. It has developed in human beings over hundreds of thousands of years and is powerful.

The stress response may save our lives when we face sudden danger, but it contributes to the increased levels of emotional distress experienced in modern life. Your mind will often trigger stress because of minor events like misplacing your mobile phone, losing internet connection, or having your credit card rejected. It can also be triggered by a memory of a previous distressing event. It is not a life-or-death situation, but your amygdala reacts as if it is. Increased stress is directly linked to many mental and physical illnesses, including increased blood pressure, heart attacks, and strokes.[9]

Because of this negativity bias, research tells us you need a minimum of three positive thoughts or emotions for every negative thought or emotion to feel that you are flourishing in life. The ratio of positive to negative thoughts or feelings in your life is called your Positivity Ratio. If you have a positivity ratio of over three to one, you will likely have flourishing mental health. If you have a ratio of less than three to one, you may have lethargic or moderate mental health; you are not ill but not mentally healthy. Drop down towards a positivity ratio of one to one and you will feel very depressed.

One of the leading researchers on the positivity ratio is Dr Barbara Fredrickson. If you visit her website (see resources at the end of the chapter), you can complete a two-minute online assessment of your own positivity ratio. She estimates that only 20 per cent of Americans score at least three to one. Thankfully your positivity ratio isn't fixed. You can improve your ratio by following the actions described in this book, especially in chapters 2, 3 and 4.

Driver 2: Develop Healthier Self-Worth

How you feel about yourself dramatically impacts your mental health. You were likely told at school that you would be happy if you worked hard and became successful. This is called eudemonic well-being and consists of two beliefs about yourself. The first belief is that you are competent as a person – that you have the ability and skills to succeed in your career and private life. This is your self-confidence, and healthy self-confidence contributes to your mental health. Issues associated with low self-confidence include Imposter Syndrome and Perfectionism. Self-confidence and how to improve it are examined in chapter 5. The second belief is that you are a person of worth. This is your self-esteem, which is how highly you value what you do and who you are in life. Unfortunately, low self-esteem often triggers feelings of shame which are destructive to your mental health.

You can improve your self-esteem by following the actions described in this book, especially in chapter 6.

Driver 3: Build And Keep Strong Connections With Those Closest To You

You need to be connected to other people to be mentally healthy – it's the survival of the species at work. As humans evolved, if you were not part of a group, your chances of survival were drastically diminished. Feelings of isolation and loneliness are your mind's warning that you are, or are becoming, dangerously disconnected from the 'group'. You can take actions that will reduce social isolation and loneliness and help build connections, as discussed in chapters 7 and 8.

Driver 4: Become More Resilient

Being mentally healthy includes being resilient. When you are resilient, you can cope with life's regular ups and downs without becoming depressed or anxious. There are two significant elements to emotional resilience. The first element is emotional recovery, or how quickly you recover after an upsetting event. You may feel upset for an hour or two if you get a parking ticket, but then you recover. It will take longer if you lose your job, but you eventually move on. The second element is sustainability, the ability to move forward during times of adversity. For example, researchers found that people with high levels of emotional resilience continued to try to solve an insoluble problem for between 100 and 150 per cent longer than those with lower resilience. Your emotional resilience is not fixed. Researchers have found that you can learn to become more resilient. We explore emotional resilience in chapter 9.

Modern Life And Your Mental Health

Unfortunately, common mental health issues such as depression and anxiety continue to increase, despite successful treatments that are widely available. The World Health Organization recently reported that due to the Covid 19 pandemic, depression and anxiety had increased by 25 per cent globally.[10] Professor Richard Davidson, Director of the Centre for Healthy Minds at the University of Wisconsin-Madison, has identified four issues in modern life that have adversely affected our mental health.[11]

Issue 1: Distractibility

At any time, just short of one in two people are distracted, not focusing on what they are doing, and are significantly less happy than those who are more focused. Mindfulness is one practice that will help reduce this happening (see chapter 3).

Issue 2: Loneliness

Researchers found that just over three out of four people described themselves as having moderate to high levels of loneliness. Loneliness predicts early death at twice the rate of obesity. Connecting to other people is critical to your mental health (see chapters 7 and 8).

Issue 3: Negative self-talk

Negative self-talk is a major trigger for depression. Mindfulness, or the practical use of metacognition, our ability to think about our thoughts and emotions, will help you to reduce negative self-talk. So will self-forgiveness and self-compassion (see chapters 2 and 8).

Issue 4: Loss of meaning or purpose in life

Having meaning or purpose in your life contributes significantly to your mental health. You can get meaning from your personal life, from the practice of religious beliefs, from your career, or other activities such as volunteering or politics. The degree to which you bring purpose into your life helps to determine how much self-esteem you have (see chapter 6).

Your Journey To Mental Health Is Yours, No One Else's

Whilst the evidence-based activities described in this book will benefit almost everyone, undertaking specific actions may be life-changing for some but have more limited benefits for others. If you are an optimistic person, you are likely to be already benefiting from your optimism. If you are pessimistic, moving towards optimism could transform your mental health. If you are someone who experiences much gratitude, you will already be benefiting from a feeling of abundance in your life. If you feel little gratitude for the things that happen to you, perhaps feeling life has short-changed you, you will find great returns from completing a gratitude diary regularly.

If you are an empathetic person who forgives those who injure you, you may already have left your hurt behind. If you feel you have been victimised and are distressed at how you were treated, then learning the process of forgiveness could free you from a constant stream of negative emotions. Everyone's journey is unique because your life circumstances and current state of mental health differ from everyone else's, even those closest to you.

Measuring Your Progress

If you find it helpful, you may want evidence that your mental health is responding to your investment using a self-reporting scale. In 2007 the National Health Service in the UK funded the development of the Warwick-Edinburgh Mental Wellbeing Scale, which is now widely used in many countries.[12] The scale consists of 14 positive statements, and you are asked to agree or disagree with each as you have experienced them over the last two weeks.[13]

For example, one of the 14 positive statements is 'I have been feeling optimistic about the future' and you self-rate yourself between 'None of the time' and 'All of the time'. It's a quick and easy tool that can be self-administered, and you can find out where to access it in the resources at the end of the chapter. Counting and recording your total score allows you to monitor change, and the guidance is that a 10 per cent change in your score in either direction is significant. Try completing it monthly when you are relaxed and have no time pressures. The maximum you can score is 70. If you score higher than 60, you are likely to be benefiting from flourishing mental health. If you score less than 44, you should talk to your doctor or health adviser – it doesn't mean you are clinically depressed, but there is a risk you could be.

Mental Illness And Mental Health

Unfortunately, you cannot be mentally healthy if you are currently suffering from a mental illness. If you are suffering from depression, anxiety, or another mental health issue, get it assessed by an appropriate health professional. Don't try to self-diagnose. Not everyone's mental health issue will meet the criteria of an illness. Estimates of illnesses vary greatly, but one objectively measurable statistic is that up to 15 per cent of the adult population will visit their doctor about mental distress in any year. Most people who receive appropriate treatment fully recover within months, usually through medication and talking therapies. The longer you leave getting help, the more risk you run of developing a second illness. For example, it is estimated that anxiety if untreated will expand to include depression 50 per cent of the time. Early diagnosis, treatment, and recovery is an effective strategy for mental health issues, the same as for physical health problems.

This book is not an alternative to proper professional support, but as you begin to recover the habits and skills described in the following chapters will support your recovery.

Summary

- Investing in your mental health today helps to protect you from mental illness in the future.
- Investing in your mental health can improve your physical health and vice versa.
- Research evidence confirms you can undertake actions that will improve your mental health.
- Modern life is hurting many people's mental health.
- Your journey towards mental health is unique.
- You can monitor your progress using scales such as the Warwick-Edinburgh Mental Wellbeing Scale.
- If you have a mental illness, get assessed and treated so you can move towards mental health.

Resources

➢Dr Barbara Fredrickson's website is www.positivityratio.com. Self-assess your positivity ratio for flourishing mental health; you are targeting 3:1 or more.

➢You can hear Dr Fredrickson explaining the Positivity Ratio at https://www.youtube.com/watch?

v=_hFzxfQpLjM

- The Warwick-Edinburgh Mental Wellbeing Scale can be printed from https://www2.uwe.ac.uk/services/Marketing/students/pdf/Wellbeing-resources/well-being-scale-wemwbs.pdf

- You can find an explanation of what it means at https://warwick.ac.uk/fac/sci/med/research/platform/wemwbs/

- You can hear Professor Davidson talking about modern life and trends in mental health at: https://www.youtube.com/watch? v=7CBfCW67xT8

Next Chapter

In chapter 2, we look at actions you can take to improve your positivity ratio by being grateful for positive things that happen in your life and learning to let go of the pain of hurtful events.

CHAPTER 2: POSITIVE EMOTIONS, THE PAST

"The past beats inside me like a second heart."

– JOHN BANVILLE

Memories of past events, recent and not-so-recent, positive and negative, often trigger strong emotions in the present. Your mind reacts to memories as if they are happening now, and that could be good news or not. You could remember a kind act from this morning or an insult from a decade ago, and your mind reacts as if it is happening right now. As discussed in chapter 1, you need to have a positivity ratio of at least three to one to achieve flourishing mental health. Your memory is an important source of both positive and negative emotions. If you can increase the number of positive emotions and reduce the number of negative emotions triggered by memories of the past, you can move towards mental health. In this chapter, we explore two human virtues, gratitude and forgiveness, which will positively affect your mental health if you can bring them into your daily life.

- ***Becoming more grateful for the positive things that have happened in your life***

A thank you text from a colleague can make you feel grateful for the recognition and change your day from bad to good. It can also make you feel pleased every time you recall that positive memory in the future. Developing gratitude in yourself is an excellent source of positive emotions. Keeping a gratitude diary is one of the simplest but most effective tools to increase the number and strength of your positive emotions, thereby improving your positivity ratio.

- ***Learning to forgive, being able to let go of the pain you feel because of the hurt you have suffered***

If a family member says something distressing to you, it can make you feel hurt. It hurts when they say it, and every time you remember them saying it. Some people revisit sad or traumatic memories more than others. They ruminate over and over about something distressing. Learning to forgive can liberate you from this stream of negative emotions. Forgiving someone is about you, not your transgressor. Forgiveness can dramatically reduce the number of negative emotions you experience, increasing your positivity ratio and supporting your journey to flourishing mental health.

Practising Gratitude Is Transformative

> *"Piglet noticed that even though he had a very small heart, it could hold a rather large amount of gratitude." – A. A. Milne*

When we feel grateful for an act of kindness, a compliment, or recognition of an accomplishment, our brain releases serotonin and dopamine. These two neurotransmitters make us feel mentally healthy. Being grateful is a natural anti-depressant and also reduces anxiety and stress. However, practising gratitude is more than just feeling grateful; it is completing an act of gratitude.

A research project at the University of California studied the effects of practising gratitude on 300 students who were suffering from anxiety or depression.[14] One group of students wrote a letter of gratitude to someone each week for three weeks; the rest did not. They found that the students who wrote the gratitude letters reported significantly improved mental health four and twelve weeks after finishing writing the letters. They also found that three months after the end of the letter writing, there was more significant brain activity when the students experienced gratitude in an fMRI scanner.

One of the surprising things they found was that you didn't need to post the letters. But you did have to write them. What was important was physically undertaking an exercise of gratitude. Dr Brene Brown, a leading researcher into shame, found that, almost without exception, the people she interviewed who expressed having joy in their life talked about regularly completing a gratitude exercise.[15]

Keeping A Gratitude Diary

Because you don't need to send the letter to trigger enhanced feelings of gratitude, you can benefit from keeping a simple gratitude diary. Each day, you list three things for which you are grateful, and that's it. Write them down on paper or type them into an app, perhaps every evening before you sleep. There are many free gratitude apps online, but you can also complete the exercise on paper. The practice is not to collect lists of positive events to review or revisit; your subconscious mind will start to do that for you. It's the exercise of identifying reasons to be grateful and combining the emotion with the physical act of recognising it.

An entry in your gratitude diary could be simple, such as "Had a good conversation with George today". You could also record the reason why the positive event happened. "I sent George a text asking how things are going". This added step shows you how often your behaviour can be the catalyst for positive events to occur in your life. Two things happen when you keep a gratitude diary for more than two weeks. Firstly, your subconscious starts to scan for positive events so that you can fill your diary. You have formed a new habit of completing the diary, and your subconscious changes its behaviour to support this new habit. By keeping a gratitude diary, your brain starts to more actively scan for positive events, not just threats, with next to no conscious effort on your part.

Another thing that happens is that when your brain notices something for which you can be grateful, your positive emotional response increases. The researchers in the University of California study were able to observe this increased brain activity in the fMRI scans of the students. The result is you feel grateful more often, and when you do, you experience a more intense positive emotion. Think of maintaining your gratitude diary as a healthy eating plan for your brain and build it into your daily routine. There are few actions you can take that are so simple and yet can reward you so quickly and consistently. If you do not currently maintain a gratitude diary, it's a great place to start your mental health journey. Just do it. There are many free gratitude apps online. Now is the time to start.

Expressing your gratitude

Researchers have identified further benefits if you express gratitude to those who have been kind or supportive. Communicating your appreciation of others can lead to new or better relationships, including romantic ones, and improved teamwork at school, university, or work. I started using a gratitude app, and after a week and a half, I noticed clear changes in myself. I have always enjoyed walking my dogs on our local beach, but I have appreciated it much more since I started using the diary. I am thankful that people turn up for my training programmes, which I took for granted before. I have noticed that I thank people in emails much more than I used to, not because I think I should but because I genuinely see the contribution others make to my work and thanking them makes me feel better. I have found that the time I invest in completing the gratitude diary is minimal, but the benefits are substantial and ongoing.

Being grateful to others is perceived as a positive quality; gratitude is rated in the top 4 per cent of admired human behaviours. People will respond positively to genuine appreciation, making you feel more connected and reducing feelings of isolation and loneliness you may have.

Forgiveness Is All About You

"To forgive is to set a prisoner free and discover that the prisoner was you." – *Lewis Smedes*

Holding a grudge has been described as drinking poison and hoping the other person dies. Forgiveness is being able to let go of your hurt. It is not about the person you're forgiving; it's about you. You are the person who is suffering every time you remember what happened. You are suffering today, and tomorrow, because of something that happened in the past. It's not diminishing or trivialising what you have experienced, but by going through a process of forgiveness described below, it may be possible to stop the hurt you are still experiencing.

You could forgive someone and decide that you will never see them again, that the relationship cannot be repaired. You could forgive someone you never knew, a stranger who hurt you and disappeared. You could forgive someone close to you who has died. You could forgive someone and repair a relationship, but forgiveness usually happens before reconciliation. They are two separate things. It's unlikely that you can genuinely reconcile with someone if you haven't been able to forgive them first. Where reconciliation is impossible, you do not need to continue feeling hurt. Forgiveness is within your power if you follow a process like Dr Luskin's nine-step process below.

Forgiveness Can Benefit Both Your Emotional And Physical Health

If someone has badly hurt you, it would not be unusual for you to ruminate about what has happened, generating a constant stream of negative emotions such as bitterness, resentment, hostility, anger, or fear. Maybe you wake up in the middle of the night, going over and over what has happened, perhaps months or years after the event. The negative emotions you associate with being hurt trigger the stress response both when it happens to you and every time you recall the memory. Your body produces increased levels of the stress hormone cortisol as if the event is happening right now. Numerous physical and emotional conditions are associated with higher cortisol levels, including the increased risk of depression, heart disease, and diabetes. Forgiveness, however, reduces your stress levels, leading to improved physical and mental health.[16]

Forgiveness can even help you to get a better night's sleep. Cortisol is your internal alarm clock. It is released into your bloodstream to wake you up. You may have noticed that many people are grumpy first thing in the morning, and that is because they are slightly stressed. Forgiveness reduces your cortisol production, allowing you to get to sleep more easily and reducing the number of times you wake up in the middle of the night, going over and over the events that are causing you distress.

Forgiveness is a process

Dr Fred Luskin is the Director of the Stanford University Forgiveness Project. He describes forgiveness as the peace and understanding that comes from lessening the blame, taking your life experience less personally, and being able to see the cost to you of holding a hurt. He has been teaching the process of forgiveness since 1999 as a means of reducing stress and improving overall mental and physical health.

I am from Northern Ireland and lived through the Troubles. I remember one of his projects, called the NI HOPE Project. In January 2000, five women, three Protestants and two Catholics from the province, all of whom had been bereaved through the murder of a close relative in the violence, travelled to Stanford for a week's training in forgiveness. When they arrived at Stanford, they completed the Degree of Hurt Measure about their loss and, on average, scored 8.6 out of 10. After their week of forgiveness training, their scores had reduced to an average of 3.6. Six months later, back in Northern Ireland, it had stabilised at 3.4. Other positive outcomes included less anger, less depression, more forgiveness, less stress, and more optimism.

Dr Luskin's Nine Steps To Forgiveness

Step 1: Be Aware Of Your Feelings

It helps if you can identify and label the feelings you are holding about the hurt you have experienced. Mindfulness, explained in the next chapter, will help you to do this. Telling your story to a small set of people you trust can also help you to understand how you feel.

Step 2: Commit to forgiveness; understand that forgiveness is for your benefit, not theirs

The process of forgiveness is to benefit you by allowing you to let the toxic emotions go. It's not to condone what they have done; you can forgive someone and at the same time decide to break all links with them.

Step 3: Do not expect reconciliation

Forgiveness is about giving you peace and freeing yourself from the toxic feelings associated with grudge-holding. Reconciliation may or may not follow from forgiveness. You can forgive someone and never see them again.

Step 4: Recognise That The Negative Event Is Past, But You Are Hurting Now

You are distressed now; your emotional and physical health is affected by the emotions triggered today. The actual event has happened, it can't be unhappened, but you can release yourself from the toxic emotions associated with the adverse event that is still hurting you today.

Step 5: Learn to reduce your stress when remembering an adverse event

Mindfulness meditation can help you to reduce your stress response. Physical activity can burn off the cortisol and adrenalin produced by your memories; you are likely to feel better after a walk because you will have reduced the cortisol level in your body.

Step 6: Focus on what you can control, abandoning unreasonable expectations of others

Often you cannot change other people's behaviour. You may feel that the other person needs to understand your hurt before you can forgive them, but that may condemn you to endless suffering. Forgiveness is about you, not them. It is not in your power to compel another person to understand things from your perspective, to apologise, or change their behaviour. However, it is within your ability to let go of the endless stream of toxic emotions associated with your hurt.

Step 7: Move on, refocus your energy on positive outcomes rather than the feeling of hurt

Change, do something different. There are things you want to achieve in your life; focus on those rather than your hurt. Learn something new, a new language, a new hobby, play a new sport, or travel more.

Step 8: Be the agent of change in your life; forgiveness is about personal empowerment

Only you can forgive. Forgiving empowers you; think of what you can achieve in the future because you are now free.

Step 9: Change the ending, positively reframing your story of being hurt

Bring this toxic emotional episode in your life to an end. You may not be able to make it right, but you can decide you will not continue to suffer. Be proud that you have the strength to let these feelings go and move on with your life. Forgiveness empowers you to move from being a victim to being a survivor. Please consider counselling if you are struggling to forgive and your memories are causing you continuing distress. A counsellor can help you to complete these steps and overcome barriers currently stopping you from releasing yourself from this pain. They are likely to have helped people who have been hurt in similar circumstances. Counsellors can be excellent coaches, helping you to benefit from changing your thoughts and behaviours.

Forgiveness Can Be The First Step To A Better Future

I was asked to deliver suicide prevention training to the senior pupils of a school outside Belfast. They were all over the age of sixteen, broadly the cut-off age for participants in suicide prevention training. The Principal met with me before the programme to discuss if one of the pupils should attend. The young man had lost his father to suicide six months previously.

Based on the school's knowledge of the young man, we agreed that he should participate if he felt it was right for him. Excluding him could trigger feelings of stigmatisation. The choice was left to him. He chose to attend. During every suicide prevention training programme, I talk about the overwhelming pain that is believed to be the emotional trigger for most suicide decisions, and the understanding that people suffering from clinical depression do not make the same choices they would make if they were not ill. The Principal met the young man afterwards to ensure he was safe and to consider if further pastoral support should be offered.

He said he was glad he had attended the programme as he now understood that his father hadn't meant to hurt him and his family. He now recognised the signs of struggle that his father had experienced before his death. The young man had been extremely angry with his father before the programme, but the anger he felt towards him had gone. Forgiveness for him was the start of a long journey of learning to live with his loss, but his journey was now possible because it started with forgiveness.

Self-Forgiveness

> *"I shouldn't have known better because I couldn't have known better, because I hadn't yet learnt what I know now. Today I forgive my younger self." – Sandy Newbigging*

Sometimes it is you who is the source of the pain. It is something you have done or not done that has caused pain and upset. Everyone makes mistakes, it's part of being human, but that doesn't mean you can simply move on and forget. You can be in denial that it happened at all. You can justify doing it because you had been hurt. You can try and suppress memories of it, or you can simply try to live with the pain.

You can also be an extremely harsh judge of your own behaviour, perhaps being less forgiving of yourself than you are of other people. Maybe you learned as a child to be self-critical. The key to self-forgiveness is being able to say honestly that you would not do the same thing today because you understand the negative impact it caused.

4Rs of self-forgiveness

Here is a four-step process that may help you to forgive yourself, reduce the pain you are in, learn from what has happened, and become a better person.

Step 1 Responsibility: accept it

Admitting what you have done is the first step towards self-forgiveness. It may be the hardest step for you. Being in denial, making excuses, or justifying your actions may mean you can't move on. Every time you remember, it generates pain, embarrassment, or feelings of low self-worth. Taking responsibility and accepting that you have engaged in actions that have hurt others or yourself allows you to start to move on.

Step 2 Remorse: allow yourself to feel guilt or remorse as a step to change

As a result of taking responsibility, you may experience a range of negative feelings, including guilt and remorse. When you've done something wrong, it's normal, even healthy, to feel guilty about it and regret it. Guilt and regret imply that you're a good person who did something bad. It's a sign of empathy and motivates you to take appropriate actions to repair or compensate for the negative impact on others.

Step 3 Restoration: if possible, make amends with whomever you've hurt, if not atone

Apologise if appropriate and look for ways to make it up to whomever you have hurt. Often relationships can be repaired and renewed if the person you have injured is open to it and you are genuinely remorseful. However, you cannot force someone to be accepting of your apology or engage further with you. That doesn't mean you can't atone for what you have done. Undertake a positive action as a substitute for restoration. Consider volunteering, donating or being kinder to other people going forward. Write a letter of apology identifying how you have harmed someone and the actions you will take to atone. Do not send the letter if it will cause further upset to the person you have injured, but commit to the actions and follow through. Trying to make amends is an integral part of forgiveness, even when the person you are forgiving is yourself. Just as you might not forgive someone else until they've made it up to you, forgiving yourself is more likely to stick when you feel like you've earned it.

Step 4 Renewal: learn from the experience and grow as a person

Everyone makes mistakes and has things for which they feel sorry or regretful. Forgiving yourself often requires finding a way to learn from the experience and grow as a person. To do this, you need to understand why you behaved the way you did and why you feel guilty. What steps can you take to prevent the same behaviours again in the future? Some of the skills contained in this book will help you to move forward; being more grateful, being mindful, being more optimistic, being a more active listener, being kinder, seeking to live a life of value, investing more in relationships, and learning how to help someone else who might be distressed will contribute to you becoming a better person. Ask yourself the question – would I do that now? The door is open to self-forgiveness if the honest answer is no. Forgive your younger self because you hadn't learnt these things yet!

Summary

- Keeping a gratitude diary is a great place to start your mental health journey.
- It works by changing how your brain operates.
- Gratitude can trigger more joy in your life.
- Forgiveness is about protecting your emotional and physical health.
- Forgiveness is letting go of your hurt.
- Forgiveness may lead to reconciliation, or it may not. It's about you, not them.
- Self-forgiveness works when you can genuinely say, "I would not do that today". Forgive your younger self.

Resources

➢ The Gratitude Garden App can be currently downloaded for free from http://www.izzymcrae.com/gratitude/

➢ I strongly recommend taking the 48 minutes necessary to watch Dr Luskin's talk to Stanford Students, "The science of happiness". It gives a great overview of an approach to life that can make you happy. It can be accessed at https://www.youtube.com/watch?v=Qvfauh-XZiQ

➢ Very powerful TEDx talk by Colleen Haggerty

who lost her leg in a car accident at age 17 and how eventually she was able to forgive the man responsible and how that affected her life, 'Forgiving the unforgiveable': https://www.youtube.com/watch?v=FE7TaUG3qQI

- A moving YouTube video of a young man's journey to forgiving his absent father, 'How forgiving my father liberated me', Agon Hare: https://www.youtube.com/watch?v=jSkoP02v7Eg

Next Chapter

In chapter 3, we explore how you can generate more positive emotions from the present. We look at mindfulness, kindness, and planning events in your day that will make you feel better.

CHAPTER 3: POSITIVE EMOTIONS, THE PRESENT

"You feel the way you do right now because of the thoughts you are thinking right now."

DR DAVID BURNS

Let me ask you a question. How do you plan to feel today? You may have a plan for today, but it's about what you will do, not how you will feel. You need to complete the school run, take the dog to the vet, prepare for a team meeting, meet a deadline for a report, hit a sales target, or make progress on a seemingly endless to-do list. It's also true that you can't plan for everything that happens in your day. But you will likely have at least an outline plan of what you need to achieve. If you don't, it could be chaotic, so you are usually proactive when considering today's actions.

It's different when it comes to how you are going to feel today. You probably consider your emotions from a reactive viewpoint. Things will happen today, and that will trigger your emotional response. If everything goes to plan, you'll feel fine. If things go wrong, your emotions may be more negative. You may become stressed if you run late for an appointment because your car has a flat tyre or if a colleague unexpectedly challenges you. Whilst you can't control every event in your day or the impact of unplanned events on your emotions, you are far from helpless. There are actions you can take and habits you can develop that will make a bad day less upsetting and a good day happier. If achieving a state of mental health is a priority for you, you can incorporate sustainable habits into your daily routine to move from languishing to flourishing mental health. You can plan that today will be an emotionally good day.

In this chapter, we are going to look at three daily

habits that you can plan into your day that will give a positive boost to your mental health:

- Be Mindful. Reduce your time on automatic pilot, being owned by your thoughts and emotions, anxious about the future or depressed about the past. Mindfulness is a well-being superpower that helps you to enjoy the day you are living as you live it.
- Be Kind. The secret to you being happier today? Be kinder. You will be happier today if you are kinder today.
- Be Happy. Invest in your mental health by doing things which trigger more positive emotions. Psychologists call it hedonic well-being; most people call it being happy.

Be Mindful

"Mindfulness is a way of befriending ourselves and our experience." –John Kabat-Zinn

Mindfulness is the practice of focusing your attention on the present moment rather than the past or future. You can think about your thoughts as you have them, metacognition, and your feelings, meta-emotion. Mindfulness helps you to use these two abilities so that your thoughts and emotions do not own you. Most people learn to be mindful through meditation. You are a physical being, as well as having thoughts and emotions. By focusing on your breathing whilst observing your thoughts and emotions, you recognise them for what they are: just thoughts and feelings which don't own you. Practising mindfulness reduces mental ill health, including depression, stress, and anxiety. A study by the University of Oxford found that after completing a mindfulness course, participants had reduced anxiety by 58 per cent, depression by 57per cent, and stress by 40 per cent.[17] Research also tells us that practising mindfulness:[18]

➢***Helps you to control your emotions***

You become better at having a thought-through response to an emotional trigger rather than an automatic, usually negative reaction, such as becoming stressed, hurt, angry, or aggressive. By learning to identify and label your thoughts and emotions, you develop your capacity to make rational decisions.

➢ ***Reduces depression***

One of the triggers for depression is rumination, going over and over in your mind about harmful incidents and reliving the emotional distress long after the incident has occurred. Practising mindfulness helps you to observe your thoughts and emotions and let them go. You become able to distinguish between yourself and what are simply mental events. You can watch and label them without harming your mental health.

➢ ***Improves your focus and memory***

When you practise mindfulness meditation, you learn to focus for a longer time. You may become a better listener because you don't become distracted; become better at completing calculations in your mind; become better at completing work-related tasks because you don't get distracted as easily. Think of mindfulness as weight training for your brain. You grow stronger neural pathways instead of muscles, but your ability to focus increases like your capacity to lift weights.

➢ ***Improves self-awareness***

You become more aware of your thoughts and emotions. Without judging yourself, you may discover how often you become irritated because of trivial events, some of which haven't happened yet. Once you observe this, you can reduce the number of times you experience unnecessary negative emotions.

Mindfulness

Mindfulness is the moment-to-moment awareness of your experiences without judgement, empowering you to let go of negative and stressful emotions. Mindfulness is being in a state of focused awareness where you are observant of your thoughts and feelings but are not controlled or overwhelmed by them. Mindfulness is about freeing your mind from your automatic emotional responses to events in your life. You have learnt to get stressed when you can't find your phone and to feel depressed when you think you are helpless to solve your problems. You can learn to observe and recognise these negative automatic responses without being owned by them. Mindfulness gives you more control over your emotions so you can make more informed choices about how you are going to act and how you are going to feel.

Mindfulness Physically Changes Your Brain

Mindfulness meditation helps you to train your conscious mind to understand the thoughts and emotions you are experiencing, even as you are experiencing them. You sit in a comfortable, relaxed position and listen to a soothing, hypnotic voice for a short period. The voice helps you to focus on your breathing whilst observing the thoughts and emotions travelling through your mind. These thoughts and feelings do not own you; as you listen to the relaxing voice, you notice the thoughts and emotions disappear. Try setting aside fifteen minutes of your day, every day, to listen to a mindfulness meditation. It's enjoyable, it's easy, but it is powerful. There are many free mindfulness meditations online. Practising mindfulness physically changes your brain. Neuroplasticity is your brain's ability to change the size of different parts of your brain in response to how you use your brain.

- ➢Mindfulness may reduce the grey matter volume of your amygdala, the stress centre of your brain.[19]

- ➢Mindfulness meditation increases the thickness of the prefrontal cortex associated with attention control so you can focus more and make rational rather than emotional decisions.[20]

- ➢Mindfulness increases the links between your prefrontal cortex and your amygdala. By practising mindfulness meditation, you may increase your control over becoming stressed.[21]

Professor Lara Boyd of the University of British Columbia is a neuroscientist. She explains neuroplasticity in her TEDx talk, “After watching this, your brain will not be the same”. The link to her talk is in the resources at the end of the chapter.

How Do You Practise Mindfulness Meditation?

Step 1: Access a mindfulness meditation on your phone or computer

There are many online resources available; many are free. The authors of "Mindfulness, A practical guide to finding peace in a frantic world" provide free meditations through their website www.franticworld.com. I use a seven-minute meditation called "Mindfulness meditation of the body and breath".

Step 2: Take 7 minutes out of your life and relax

Listen to the meditation whilst relaxing. Learn to focus on physical sensations whilst simultaneously identifying your thoughts and emotions. This is practising the skill of metacognition, humans' ability to think about their thoughts and feelings as they think or feel them.

Step 3: That's it

The 7 minutes relaxes you and reduces stress. It develops your ability to identify and label thoughts and emotions that may be damaging your mental health. This is the first step to reframing internal negative self-talk statements about guilt, low self-esteem, stress, forgiveness, low self-confidence and many other mental health issues. These are explained later in this book.

Mindful Activities

You can benefit from mindfulness whilst undertaking other activities besides meditation. You may find swimming to be a mindful activity. It is an aerobic exercise which contributes to your physical well-being but is also beneficial for your mental health. You are in a silent world where you watch the bubbles when you exhale, timing every stroke to ensure your mouth and nose are out of the water when you breathe in and watching your fingers reach out to propel yourself forward. By the time you finish swimming, you often will have forgotten the irritations and annoyances in your life, and the cortisol level in your body will be substantially reduced. If I go swimming today, I will improve my positivity ratio and feel great for hours, if not days. Find what works best for you and plan it into your week. And then your emotions are not solely reactive to events; you are proactively planning how you will feel.

Many people use running or cycling as a mindful activity, but not all mindful activities need to be that energetic. Walking your dog on the beach can be a mindful activity, and sitting on a chair in the sunshine while reading a book can be a mindful activity as well. Many people mention crocheting or knitting as an activity which supports their mental health; find what works for you and build it into your day.

Be Kind

"Three things in human life are important: The first is to be kind. The second is to be kind. And the third is to be kind." – Henry James

Do you want to know the secret to being happier today? Be kinder today. It's often as simple as that. A Japanese study has found that happy people become happier through acts of kindness:[22] You become happier by counting your own acts of kindness and happy people are more motivated to perform acts of kindness. Researchers have found that performing acts of kindness for seven days will make you happier; the more acts you complete, the happier you will be. And they found that it doesn't matter if you perform acts of kindness for your family, strangers, or yourself: kindness just works.[23]

Kindness Is Good For Everyone

"The greatest work that kindness does to others is that it makes them kind themselves." – Amelia Earhart

Being kind to someone makes you feel better. It

makes the person you are kind to feel better. It even makes someone who observes you being kind feel better. And it also increases the chance that the observer of your act of kindness will carry out an act of kindness themselves.[24]Being kind makes you feel better because it triggers dopamine production in your brain. Dopamine provides an intense feeling of pleasure and reward. You may have heard the term 'helper's high' – that is the dopamine effect. Being kind also builds your sense of belonging and reduces feelings of isolation by producing oxytocin. Oxytocin is sometimes referred to as the love hormone, as it plays a significant role in mother/baby bonding. Oxytocin also helps to lower your blood pressure and reduce stress and anxiety whilst increasing pain tolerance.

Being kind reduces depression. Researchers found that training people to be kinder over three weeks significantly reduced depression two months later for almost everyone. What might surprise you is that the least agreeable people, based on the Big Five Inventory Personality Test, benefited the most from the kindness training.[25]So even if you are currently a curmudgeon or a grinch, developing your kindness muscle will generate more positive emotions, moving you towards happiness and mental health. If you practise kindness, it will make your bad days better and your good days great.

Becoming Kinder

Kindness is both an emotional state and an action. Kind people are predisposed to help. Kind people are more aware of other people's needs and are more likely to consider an act that benefits others, not themselves. Kind people may be described as helpful, generous, friendly, warm-hearted, and compassionate. Kind people also do acts of kindness. An act of kindness is doing something beneficial for another person, group of people, or community with no expectation of a payback. The act of kindness is an end in itself. Here are five steps you can follow to help you become kinder.

- **Step 1: Become a better listener.**

Hearing is not listening. You need to clear your mind and listen to what someone is trying to say to you. To improve your listening skills, listen as if you are going to be tested on what someone has just said. Could you summarise what has been said to you? Sometimes all someone needs from you is that you let them speak and you hear what they say. Ask questions about what the person says instead of telling them what to do. Really listening to someone is being kind.

- **Step 2: Become a conscientious observer.**

It's important that we understand as much as possible about the person and their circumstances:

communication is not just verbal. We may realise someone is upset because of their body language or that they're stressed because they are digging their nails into their palms, even if at the same time they have a smile. Investing time in understanding someone is being kind.

- **Step 3: Learn empathy.**

Step into their world and see it as they see it. Empathy is not sympathy, nor is it providing advice or solutions. Empathy is often the first step in kindness, taking the time to see the world as someone else sees it. Walk a mile in someone's shoes and know why their feet hurt.

- **Step 4: Be sincere.**

Kindness is about giving, not receiving. Being kind so that people will be responsive to your needs is manipulative and not genuine kindness. An act of kindness is done solely to help someone else.

- **Step 5: Consistent acts of kindness.**

Be generous with your time, with your listening, with your empathy, with your gratitude, with your resources. Be kind to a wide range of people, not just those close to you. Be kind to yourself; treat yourself the same as you would treat a friend. Make kindness a habit; do one kind thing a day and see the positive changes in your life.

Be Happy

"We hold these truths to be self-evident, that all men are created equal, that they are endowed by their Creator with certain unalienable Rights, that among these are Life, Liberty and the pursuit of Happiness." – American Declaration of Independence

If you offered a group of people one wish for themselves, many, if not most, would choose to be happier. If you asked them what they would choose for their children, happiness usually comes before success or wealth. The writers of the Declaration of Independence used the word happiness in the same manner as most people outside the field of psychology use it – in its broadest sense. Emotions such as pride, contentment, excitement, amusement, satisfaction, and relief; all can fit under the broad emotional umbrella of being happy.

Psychologists will tell you that you cannot be happy all the time. That is not news to anyone I know. They will also tell you that trying too hard to be happy may make you unhappy. I don't know many people who try too hard to be happy, but I know many who feel guilty doing something they enjoy. Your parents and teachers likely told you that working hard, passing your exams, and having a successful career will make you happy. Success leads to happiness. Except it's not as simple as that. You will know someone who is successful in life but isn't happy. Maybe that describes you. Your life may be proceeding broadly as planned, but you don't feel happy, certainly not the way you had imagined when you were younger. There is evidence that happiness, rather than being a product of success, actually supports the achievement of success. Research has established that happier people tend to be more successful across multiple measures in life, including marriage, friendship, income, work performance, and health.[26]

Do Things You Enjoy; Be Happier

"What day is it?" "It's today", squeaked Piglet.
"My favourite day," said Pooh. – A.A. Milne

Walking on a beach, watching a great football match, and meeting your friends for a meal and a glass of wine are all pleasurable activities and add to your sense of happiness. This is called hedonic well-being; doing things you enjoy makes you happier and emotionally healthier. The activities that are going to make you feel happy are individual to you. However, researchers have identified the activities that work best for most people. To study everyday happiness, researchers at the London School of Economics in a project called "Mappiness" created a smartphone app that 'dinged' people at random points during the day. The app asked participants how they felt and what they were doing that was causing them to feel that way.[27]Here are the top 10 activities that made people happy, and the percentage of increased happiness reported:

1. Intimacy, making love:14.20%
2. Theatre, dance, concert:9.29%
3. Exhibition, museum, library:8.77%
4. Sports, running, exercise:8.12%
5. Gardening, allotment:7.83%
6. Singing, performing:6.95%
7. Talking, chatting, socialising:6.38%
8. Birdwatching, nature watching:6.28%
9. Walking, hiking:6.18%
10. Hunting, fishing:5.82%

Working hard, doing your taxes, finalising reports, and catching up with your emails unsurprisingly didn't make the top 10! Life will distract you easily if you do not plan your hedonic moments. You can see the value of socialising with your colleagues during the coffee break rather than sending an extra email, but which action did you choose yesterday? You know how much more beneficial it is for your mental health to take your dog for a walk than to stay late to finish a report, but which have you planned for tomorrow? Hedonic activities will make you feel better, generating more positive emotions and contributing to moving your positivity ratio above three to one. How many of these activities are you planning for your day? Proactively planning positive events and activities will help you to achieve mental health and feel happier.

Minimise Activities Which Trigger Negative Emotions

There are, of course, activities that make us feel bad; they generate stress, annoyance, and feelings of exhaustion and damage our positivity ratio. According to the Mappiness project, here are the most negative activities that will diminish your happiness:

1. Sick in bed: -20.4%
2. Working, studying: -5.43%
3. Care or help for adults: -4.30%
4. Waiting, queueing: -3.51%
5. Admin, finances, organising: -2.45%
6. In a meeting, seminar, or class: -1.50%
7. Travelling, commuting: -1.47%

If being stuck in a traffic jam daily makes you feel depressed, it may be less of a mental health issue and more of a planning issue. Think of the day you have planned for tomorrow. Can you add one hedonic activity and remove one unhappy one? Can you reclaim some time from the negative side of life and replace it with an emotionally positive event? Remember that to have flourishing mental health you need a positivity ratio of at least three to one.

Change the activities in your day, and you change your positivity ratio.

Summary

- Be Mindful. Mindfulness is truly a mental health superpower. It physically shrinks your brain's stress centre and reduces depression, anxiety, and stress.
- Be Kind. Kindness is the gateway to happiness. Practise it consistently, and it will make you happier.
- Be Happy. Invest in activities that make you happy today, not just things that make you feel better tomorrow. As John Lennon said, "Life is what happens to you while you're busy making other plans".

Resources

➢"Mindfulness, a practical guide to finding peace in a frantic world" written by Professor Mark Williams and Dr Danny Penman. Free mindfulness meditations through their website www.franticworld.com.

➢Professor Williams explains the science behind mindfulness (4 minutes): Trigger warning he talks a little bit about thoughts of suicide:
https://www.youtube.com/watch?v=8GVwnxkWmSM

➢I recommend a 13-minute video by Professor Shauna Shapiro of Santa Clara University called "The Power of Mindfulness: What you practise grows stronger". You can find it at https://www.youtube.com/watch?v=IeblJdB2-Vo.

- ➢Excellent 3-minute explanation of the psychology behind mindfulness: https://www.youtube.com/watch?v=w6T02g5hnT4

- ➢Great 4-minute video/cartoon about how our brains are built to be kind by Professor Dacher Keltner of UC Berkeley: https://www.youtube.com/watch?v=SsWs6bf7tvI

- ➢Dr Lara Boyd's TEDx talk, "After watching this, your brain will not be the same". Explains neuroplasticity and can be found at: https://www.youtube.com/watch?v=LNHBMFCzznE

- ➢Does success lead to happiness, or does happiness lead to success? Light-hearted but semi-scientific demonstration and explanation: "Why happy people do it better, the science of happiness": https://www.youtube.com/watch?v=IkMHZ7mchVo

Next Chapter

The most accurate predictor that you are going to become depressed when something goes wrong in your life is your level of pessimism before the adverse event happens. Pessimism damages your mental health, but you can learn how to neutralise it and become more optimistic. We explain how in chapter 4.

CHAPTER 4: POSITIVE EMOTIONS, THE FUTURE

"Optimism is the faith that leads to achievement. Nothing can be done without hope and confidence."

– HELEN KELLER

When delivering mental health training for members of the veterinary profession, I ask the participants what the difference is between being an optimist and a pessimist. The answer is usually the same: the optimist sees a glass half full whilst the pessimist sees a glass half empty. But that's not technically correct. If the glass is half full, that is a factual statement, not an optimistic statement. If the glass is half empty, that is also a factual statement, not a pessimistic statement. If you are an optimist, you see the world with a positive psychological bias. You see it in a better light than it is. You will look at the glass and may subconsciously estimate it is more than half full. If you are a pessimist, the opposite is true. You see the world in a lesser light than it is. You look at the glass and may estimate that it is less than half full. Pessimism is a negative psychological bias.

We use our psychological bias to explain why things happen in our life: we have either an optimistic or pessimistic explanatory style. Researchers have found that the optimistic explanatory style discussed below leads to materially better life outcomes than the pessimistic one. Optimists live longer than pessimists, earn more money, are more successful, and have better relationships. A veterinary nurse said to me during a programme that she felt comfortable as a pessimist, not expecting too much from life. She didn't want to be flattened when things went wrong; if she expected the worst, then life would turn out to be better than she expected. Sadly, for her, in practice, her strategy is highly unlikely to be successful. Researchers have found substantial evidence that pessimists experience more problems and disappointments in life than optimists. Pessimism is directly linked to depression; the pessimist subconsciously contributes to increasing the risk that when something negative happens in their life, they will respond by becoming depressed.

Benefits Of Being An Optimist

The evidence is that being an optimist, rather than a pessimist, is better for your physical health, mental health, personal life, and work life.

➢ ***Being more optimistic is good for your mental health***

Optimism reduces the chance that you will become depressed and the severity of its impact if you do. A study of Australian pupils found that the most optimistic group had half the risk of becoming depressed compared to the most pessimistic group.[28] If you are more optimistic, you will also be more resilient when things do go wrong in your life.[29] If you have higher levels of pessimism, you will have more severe depressive symptoms if you become depressed.[30] Pessimism can also make you more anxious and reduce your quality of life.[31]

➢ ***Being more optimistic is good for your physical health***

In a study of over 70,000 nurses, researchers found that the most optimistic nurses were almost 30 per cent less likely to die of any cause over the six years studied than the most pessimistic nurses.[32]A study by the University of Kentucky on members of the School Sisters of Notre Dame found that the most optimistic nuns outlived the most pessimistic nuns by an average of ten years.[33] In the Netherlands, a study of over 1000 older individuals found that participants who had reported higher levels of optimism were 55 per cent less likely to die from any cause during the study.[34]

➢ ***Being more optimistic is good for your career and personal life***

Ten years after graduation, US law students who were optimistic in their first year earned an average of $32,667 more than their pessimistic peers.[35] Optimistic insurance sales agents sold 37 per cent more insurance in their first two years of service than pessimistic agents and remained in their job at twice the rate.[36]If you are an optimist, you are likely to be a better problem solver than a pessimist, leading to more positive and happy relationships.[37] If you are in a romantic relationship, and at least one of you is optimistic, both of you will likely benefit from a higher-quality and longer-lasting relationship.[38] Be more optimistic to be more attractive to your romantic partner. People found their partners to be more attractive when they exhibited optimistic behaviour.[39]

Optimism

Optimism is having a positive psychological bias that influences how we explain things that happen to us, the decisions we make, and how we predict and create the future.

➢ ***Explaining things that happen to us***

Optimism is an explanatory style.[40] You have a preferred way of explaining to yourself the reason why something has happened. This explanatory style is either optimistic or pessimistic.

If you are an optimist, you explain good things happening in your life in a positive way:

> **Permanence:** the reason the good thing happened to you is permanent and will continue. You passed your exam because you are clever, and you will continue to pass exams.
>
> **Pervasive:** the reason the good thing happened to you repeats itself across different areas of your life. You are good at doing lots of things because you work hard.
>
> **Personal:** the good thing happened because of you. You're clever and a hard worker.

When something terrible happens to an optimist, they explain it in reverse.

> **Temporary**: I failed my exam because I didn't study hard enough. I will pass it the next time.

Specific: I hate chemistry, and the teacher is boring.

Non-personal: Half the class failed; the exam was just too hard.

The adverse event is temporary and will not repeat, it happened for a specific reason and is not a total disaster, and it doesn't make you a failure.

➢ ***The decisions we make***

"Whether you think you can or you can't, you're right." – Henry Ford

As mentioned above, optimistic nurses were 30 per cent less likely to die from any cause than their pessimistic colleagues over a six-year period. A significant reason for this was the positive, optimistic decisions they made in their life. If you were one of the optimistic nurses, you were more likely to decide to go for a walk because you would feel better afterwards or go swimming because it is a mindful activity that is great for your mental health. You would more often seek help when you are struggling with a problem because it helps you achieve a positive outcome. There would be an increased chance you would stop smoking because you don't want to develop lung cancer, and you would eat a healthier diet because you want to avoid multiple health risks.

If you are an optimist, you will make more positive decisions because you believe your choices will lead to more positive outcomes; you are motivated towards success. Pessimists are motivated away from failure. This is not negative if you understand how it affects your decision-making; unfortunately, many pessimists make decisions subconsciously and miss out on many of life's opportunities.

➢ ***Predicting and creating the future***

"What would you attempt to do if you knew you would not fail?" – Robert H. Schuller

Will you apply for a promotion? Will you open a new business? Will you ask someone out on a date? What you choose to do will be influenced by what you predict the future outcome will be. If you are an optimist, you will see yourself succeeding before you even start, not based on evidence but on your optimistic bias. You are more likely to try something new and continue to strive for success for longer.

Becoming More Optimistic

The choice would therefore appear simple; you should just choose to be more optimistic. The reality is, of course, that it's not that simple. Imagine you are feeling depressed and you ask a friend for help. They tell you that all you need to do to stop feeling depressed is to make yourself feel better. It's not advice you are likely to value. Advising someone to become more optimistic is also overly simplistic and perhaps unhelpful. There are many reasons you may be a pessimist, and there are barriers and limitations to how optimistic you can become. Your genes may make you more pessimistic than your family, friends, or colleagues. Estimates vary greatly, but at least 25 per cent of your emotional makeup is genetic, so there is a point where you can't become more optimistic.

What happens to you in life also affects your level of optimism. If you have suffered trauma or repeated disappointments in your life, then you may have learned lessons that will consciously and subconsciously affect many of the future decisions you make. Your pessimism may be ingrained, and you may need the support of a therapist to change; many pessimists have worked with a therapist as a coach and benefited greatly. If one of your parents was a pessimist, you might have started to learn pessimistic thought patterns as soon as you began to understand speech. Your automatic subconscious pessimistic thought patterns may seem normal and natural to you; so natural you don't even know they're there and influencing many of the decisions you make. These negative learned thought patterns are problematic, but they also offer great potential for positive change in your life. Pessimism and optimism are on a continuum, with pessimism at one end and optimism at the other. You can take practical, proven steps to move along the scale towards the optimistic end. Even if you are limited in how far you can progress, you can benefit greatly from moving towards the optimistic end of the scale. Here are five steps that can help you move towards being more optimistic:

Step 1: Find out how optimistic or pessimistic you are

You can find out how optimistic or pessimistic you are by completing a free online Optimism Test through the University of Pennsylvania.[41] Register and complete the online questionnaire and receive an instant assessment against each element of pessimism, see resources at end of the chapter.

Step 2: Identify the pessimistic thoughts in your mind

Mindfulness meditation will help significantly with this step. If you learned pessimism from a parent, you might be so used to your pessimistic thought process that it's automatic and below your conscious awareness. Using mindfulness meditation, you learn to identify that a thought is a pessimistic thought; mindfulness trains your mind to accept that that's all it is, a thought. It doesn't own you, and you do not have to follow its pathway. You can say to yourself, "I notice that I am thinking this negative thought," and you can label it as a pessimistic thought. One mindfulness exercise is to imagine your pessimistic thoughts queueing at a bus stop, and a bus pulls up. They get on, and the bus drives away, but you don't. They don't own you.

Step 3: Challenge the pessimistic thoughts that cause you a negative bias[42]

When you can identify pessimistic thoughts through mindfulness meditation, challenge them with the question, "What evidence do you have that this is an accurate assessment or prediction?" When you challenge your pessimistic thought, it often loses its power because there is no substance to it. You are moving from making decisions based on a negative psychological bias to an evidence-based, objective decision called appraisal.

A negative thought isn't a pessimistic thought if there is evidence to support it. For example, a little voice saying don't stand in the middle of the road because you might get hit by a car isn't pessimism, because it's based on evidence. Challenge the thought and collect evidence, then decide; that decision may or may not be different, but it will be an evidence-supported decision rather than a pessimistically biased decision.

Step 4: Neutralise your pessimistic distortions

We all have habits that are called cognitive distortions, damaging psychological shortcuts. These distortions include:

- **Catastrophising**. Making negative mountains out of molehills. You are likely to catastrophise when you have higher levels of cortisol, the stress hormone, in your bloodstream. If you identify that you are catastrophising, step away, go for a walk, and don't make any decision until you have gathered evidence. You can then make a more informed, realistic decision when you are less stressed. I never respond immediately to emails that irritate me, even though emotionally that's what I want to do. I consciously park my response until my cortisol level returns to normal, and I find that in most cases, I have catastrophised something of no consequence.

- **All-or-nothing thinking**. If it's not perfect, it's useless. Life is rarely all or nothing. You may struggle to achieve something worthwhile, but don't let that pessimistic voice in your head make you give up trying. Things are rarely perfect in life, but they don't need to be for you to move forward and achieve things. If you are a pessimist, you tend to focus on risk and failure. Try to identify when you have these thoughts, recognise they are pessimistic distortions, and let them get on the bus and drive off.

- **Seeing things as absolutes.** Everybody knows, everybody agrees. Actually, not everybody knows, and not everybody agrees. Often if you have an absolute thought, it isn't based on facts and has a negative distortion. Ask yourself, "What's the evidence to support this extreme statement?" Usually, the thought loses its power over you.

- **Using negative filters**. Pessimists often unconsciously search for evidence to support their negative predictions and ignore evidence supporting a more positive outcome. Keep checking for your negative bias: don't go with your initial gut feeling. Ask yourself if you have gathered all the appropriate evidence available – get into the habit of writing down the evidence for and against a decision and then make a more informed choice.

- **Jumping to conclusions not supported by evidence.** Leonardo Da Vinci advised us to be comfortable with confusion. Often, anxiety will drive you to make a quick, uninformed decision based on subconscious automatic thought patterns rather than facts. The universe and your mind don't like vacuums, so we often jump to conclusions unsupported by evidence. Practice delaying decisions until you have gathered sufficient evidence to make a more rational and unbiased decision. Initially, you may find that you feel stressed about not making a quick decision, but focus on gathering the evidence, and with repetition, it can become a habit.

Step 5: Practise optimistic reframing particularly if you are a pessimist

A little voice in your head telling you that you will fail often leads to failure: you just give up. To reduce the impact of this negative self-talk, start by following one simple rule: Don't say anything to yourself that you wouldn't say to someone you liked. Be kinder to yourself. Practise using the optimistic explanatory style, as it will lead to substantially improved life outcomes even if you are a pessimist. It is not naive Pollyanna thinking. It helps to ensure you do not make bad emotionally biased choices before you have the chance to collect the evidence and make a rational informed decision.

Pessimistic Thought: I'm going to be expelled from University because I'm not clever enough.

Gather evidence: I passed the entrance exams; I haven't failed any exams; I'm not the worst or best in my class.

Optimistic Thought: I am struggling at the moment, things will get better; I'm not in danger of being expelled, I am struggling to adjust to university life; I am not the only student struggling.

As you can see, the reframed optimistic self-talk isn't unrealistic thinking. It's not unicorns and rainbows. It's simply moving from a negative emotional bias to a more objective, realistic and productive approach.

One Size Does Not Fit All

Imagine you are at a sales team meeting. Your sales manager announces that the company is changing its bonus system. Your sales target is increasing by 25 per cent, but so is your sales commission. If your immediate thought is about a new car, you are likely an optimist; if your first thought is about a new job, you are likely a pessimist. If you are the sales manager, your first thought might be that you should consider becoming more empathetic.

What motivates one person could easily act as a disincentive for someone else. I would describe myself as a realistic pessimist; other people in the charity are optimists. The difference is apparent when setting a budget for the year ahead. I always start with a minimum budget, asking what income we need to generate to cover next year's costs. Until I am comfortable that we can achieve this minimum budget, I find it challenging to look at new or expanded projects. This is because, as a pessimist, I am strongly motivated away from failure. Once I am confident that we will achieve the minimum budget, I am open to new and exciting projects. But not before! My colleagues understand this process and that it doesn't take that long. They also know that I become fully committed to delivering the minimum budget and exciting new projects. And I will not fail.

Optimism Is Self-Fulfilling And Beneficial In Itself

Why is there such a difference between life outcomes for optimists and pessimists? Dr Tali Sharot, Professor of Cognitive Neuroscience at University College London, explains in an excellent TEDx video why this happens based on her research findings, see the link in the resources section at the end of this chapter.

1. The optimistic explanatory style is emotionally positive, today! You can look forward to better times, you box in the negatives of the situation, and you don't feel shame because you made a mistake. The pessimistic explanatory style simply makes you feel worse than you need to feel.
2. People with high expectations always feel better. You feel better right now if you expect to have success in the future no matter what actually happens. Remember the quote from Dr Burns of Stanford University, "You feel the way you do right now because of the thoughts you are thinking right now" (see chapter 3). If you think you are going to succeed in the future, you feel positive emotions right now which contribute to moving your positivity ratio towards three to one.

3. Optimism makes you try harder. Optimism leads to success across multiple life measures in both mental and physical health.

Optimism is a psychological bias. This keeps optimists optimistic in the face of evidence to the contrary. As Dr Sharot explains in her TEDx video, if an optimist estimates the chance of developing cancer over their lifetime is 10 per cent, when they are faced with evidence that it is actually 30 per cent, they will adjust, but not to 30 per cent, but maybe to 11 per cent. However, if they originally estimated a 50 per cent chance of developing cancer over their lifetime, when shown evidence that it is actually 30 per cent, they make a far bigger adjustment towards the more positive figure – they now estimate their chances at perhaps 35 per cent.

Can You Be Too Optimistic?

Yes. Optimism is a psychological bias, and unrealistic optimism can cause you problems. In 1995, a man called McArthur Wheeler committed an armed robbery on two banks in Pittsburgh, Pennsylvania. Later the same day, the police arrested him at his home, brought him to the local station, and started interrogating him. McArthur Wheeler asked the police how they had caught him so quickly, and they showed him a picture from the first bank's surveillance system. He expressed his surprise as he explained that he had been wearing cold lemon juice on his face. Cold lemon juice was used as invisible ink by spies in the Middle Ages, so McArthur Wheeler convinced himself that he was invisible when he rubbed the cold lemon juice on his face.

Two research psychologists, Dunning and Kruger, from Cornel University, read about this and came up with a theory: to know that you are one of the worst bank robbers in history, you need some basic knowledge and skills of being a bank robber. McArthur Wheeler had no knowledge or skills around robbing a bank, so his unrealistic optimism told him he would be a successful bank robber and solve all his money problems. If they were right in their theory, Dunning and Kruger would find the same pattern of behaviour repeated in a group of people. They asked their students at Cornel to predict how well they would do in their upcoming exams, and then they compared predicted scores against actual scores. The results were emphatic. The students who had invested heavily in their studies scored highest in their exams but were also remarkably accurate in their predictions. The students who did not study as hard scored lower, but their predictions were wildly over-optimistic – they predicted they would do as well, if not better, as the best-performing students. It's called the Dunning Kruger Effect.[43] Unrealistic optimism will get you into situations where you will ask what possessed you to think this was a good idea. So be an optimist, but think about risk and opportunity and gather the necessary evidence before making big decisions in your life. Optimists are motivated towards success, but that doesn't mean you should ignore risks. Pessimists are motivated away from failure, but that doesn't mean you should ignore opportunities.

Summary

- Pessimism is harmful to your mental and physical health.
- It is primarily a learned behaviour that can be changed.
- Use mindfulness meditation to help you identify your pessimistic thoughts.
- Challenge your pessimistic thoughts and ask them for evidence to support what they are saying.
- Make your decision based on the evidence, and then drive forward to achieving your goal.

Resources

- Martin Seligman's book, *Learned Optimism: How to Change your Mind and your Life*, is a must-read if you want to understand pessimism and its connection to mental health issues such as depression. It is a very accessible book and it does what it says on the cover; if you are a pessimist, it could change your life.
- Do the Optimism Test at the University of Pennsylvania's Authentic Happiness Questionnaire Centre: https://www.authentichappiness.sas.upenn.edu/testcenter

- ➢Listen to Dr Seligman defining Optimism in less than 2 minutes: https://www.youtube.com/watch?v=8-rMuJW-UKg

- ➢Very short video of Simon Sinek explaining what optimism means to him: https://www.youtube.com/watch?v=lcja1Hi39aQ

- ➢Brilliant TEDx talk by Dr Tali Sharot, a neuroscientist and Professor of Cognitive Neuroscience at University College London who explains the optimism bias, what it is and why it makes us happier and healthier: https://www.youtube.com/watch?v=B8rmi95pYL0

Next Chapter

Healthy self-confidence is a significant contributor to mental health. Your self-confidence is your assessment of how competent you are to succeed in life. Unfortunately for many, there can be a discrepancy between how competent you are and how competent you feel. This can give rise to issues such as Impostor Syndrome.

CHAPTER 5: HEALTHY SELF-CONFIDENCE

"What lies behind us and what lies before us are tiny matters compared to what lies within us." – Ralph Waldo Emerson

When you were at school, your teachers and parents encouraged you to work hard and do well in your exams or assessments so that ideally you could pursue a successful career and ultimately live a happy and fulfilling life. This approach supports the development of two critical elements of your mental health: self-confidence and self-esteem. We examine self-esteem, your belief that you are living a life of value, in chapter 6. This chapter examines self-confidence, your belief that you are competent to succeed in life.

Benefits Of Healthy Self-Confidence

There are many practical benefits of healthy self-confidence, including:

- **Self-confidence helps you to make safer decisions**

When we have a healthy self-confidence, we are more likely to establish appropriate boundaries that keep us safe. It's easier to say no to people if you have confidence in your decisions.

- **Self-confidence helps you to make decisions and stick with them**

"Self-confidence is the first requisite to great undertakings." – Samuel Johnson

Self-confidence tells you that you're good at making the right decisions in life, so you are more likely to make a decision and stick with it. This reduces procrastination and increases your sustainability. When things get difficult, you are less likely to give up.

- **Self-confidence helps you to be more resilient**

Resilience helps you to continue forward when there are barriers in your road and pick yourself up emotionally after a failure. Self-confidence enables you to drive through obstacles because you believe you have made the right decision.

- **Self-confidence allows for failure**

Samuel Beckett said, "Ever tried, ever failed? No matter, try again, fail again, fail better". Healthy self-esteem allows for failure; success often comes after many less successful attempts.

- **Self-confidence improves your relationships**

If you have healthy self-confidence, you don't need to constantly seek approval from your family, friends, or romantic partners. Do you have a friend who always seems self-confident? Do you notice how they find it easy to draw firm boundaries and have relationships with people who are good for them?

- **Self-confidence helps you to be a better communicator**

Someone with healthy self-confidence is likely to be more open in expressing their ideas in a straightforward, direct manner, reducing the chances of miscommunication and confusion. Unfortunately, people with lower levels of self-confidence may not feel able to speak up, leading to an absence of understanding.

➢ **Self-confidence often triggers respect**

People are more likely to respond positively if you act confidently. They often accept your judgement that you know what you're doing. Leaders are usually confident about themselves and their ideas, and often people accept their assessments as factual.

➢ **Self-confidence can reduce anxiety**

Anxiety is your concern about adverse events that may happen in the future. Healthy self-confidence helps you to see yourself succeeding in the future, reducing your anxiety around failure.

➢ **Self-confidence helps you to achieve your goals**

> *"Believe you can, and you're halfway there." – Theodore Roosevelt*

Part of healthy self-confidence is remembering your previous successes, which encourages you to pursue and deliver further success. Believing you can succeed enables you to keep going even if things are not going your way.

➢ **Self-confidence contributes to your self-esteem**

Self-confidence is key to success, and what you achieve in your life impacts how you value yourself. The more success you have, the more self-esteem you may feel. Self-confidence and self-esteem are different but overlapping beliefs that form a significant portion of your mental health.

Problems With Low Self-Confidence

Low levels of self-confidence, unfortunately, turn the above benefits into problems, sometimes problems that significantly impact your quality of life:

- You are likely to have fewer and weaker boundaries and may be more susceptible to peer pressure.

- You may experience more procrastination, and even when you make a decision, you are more likely to change your mind.

- You are likely to be less resilient, taking longer to recover from failures, and more likely to give up when you don't immediately succeed.

- You may have fewer healthy relationships, weaker boundaries, and be more dependent on others' approval for your self-worth.

- Less confident communication can lead to confusion and damaged relationships.

- You will be ignored or dismissed more often because people pick up that you are not confident of your ability to succeed.

- ➢You are likely to have higher anxiety levels because, internally, you have a voice telling you that you will fail.

- ➢You are likely to fail more often in life: having a negative assessment of your chances of success tends to be self-fulfilling.

- ➢Fewer successes and more failures in life will harm your self-worth.

Low self-confidence can damage your mental health, but your low self-confidence often results from learned behaviours that you can change. You can take actions that lead to healthier self-confidence.

Self-Confidence

Self-confidence is your belief that you have the necessary skills, knowledge, and sustainability to successfully meet the needs of your life. Elements of self-confidence include:[44]

You believe you are a good problem solver

Believing you can overcome problems you face in life that are stopping you from achieving your goals is self-confidence. Some self-confidence is task-specific; for example, you may be confident that you can drive a car because you do it every day without crashing. But self-confidence can also be more global; you may also believe you could learn to drive a tractor because you were able to learn to drive a car. Self-confidence includes believing you are good at solving problems and learning new things. Researchers have found that self-confidence is important for learning. It is difficult to change intelligence, but self-confidence can be improved, leading to better learning outcomes.

You believe that you can successfully make decisions and act on your own

There are often occasions when you need to make a decision and act on it. People with healthy self-confidence are more likely to feel comfortable doing so and, therefore, more likely to be successful. For example, researchers have found that student nurses with higher levels of self-confidence perform better when they go on duty in hospitals for the first time. This is because they can better implement what they have learned in theory into practice, even in stressful circumstances.[45]

You believe you have a track record of success

Success and self-confidence occur in a constantly self-reinforcing cycle that empowers further success. If you have high levels of self-confidence, you may also be better at remembering and recalling occasions when you succeeded.

You feel able to express your opinion

Self-confidence is not just internal: you communicate your self-confidence to other people. You are more likely to speak up at a meeting and express your point of view if you have healthy self-confidence.

Becoming More Self-Confident

"It is not the mountain we conquer but ourselves." – Sir Edmund Hillary

Your self-confidence is not fixed: you can build your self-confidence in many different ways. Here we set out some strategies and habits you can develop.

➢**Nothing succeeds like success**

Completing a difficult or new task boosts self-confidence and primes you to attempt more projects in the future. Setting and achieving goals, big or small, can positively impact your self-confidence. Deciding you will go swimming three times a week and accomplishing that goal will benefit your physical and emotional well-being and build your self-confidence. Set big and small goals in different parts of your life, and then pursue them and celebrate your achievements.

➢**Copying others with healthy self-confidence**

We often copy those closest to us when we are young and trying to work out how to make our way in the world. But age shouldn't be a barrier to doing this: we can copy self-confidence from role models at any age. If you admire someone, ask yourself what they would do. Some characteristics that we might copy from others with healthy self-confidence may include celebrating other people's success, being open-minded, being optimistic, being willing to take risks, being prepared to laugh at ourselves, being decisive, always learning and growing, admitting rather than hiding mistakes, and accepting appropriate responsibility for their actions.

➢ **Positive and supportive encouragement**

Someone being supportive in your life can make a huge difference. Having a coach or a mentor can bring about success that might not be achieved on your own. Having someone encouraging you to stick at it through a difficult time could make the difference between success and failure. If you have someone who likes to criticise you, strengthen your boundaries with them; whatever they are getting out of it, there is a cost to you.

➢ **Your physical and mental health**

If you are physically well, you are likely to be more self-confident than if you are suffering from an illness or injury. Getting sufficient sleep supports healthy self-confidence. Investing in other elements of your mental health will positively impact your self-confidence. Practising forgiveness, mindfulness, consistent kindness, and becoming more optimistic will positively impact your self-confidence.

- **Read every day, watch TEDx talks, watch the History Channel, and learn something every day**

Try to learn something every day of your life. It means you know more when you go to bed than when you get up. Learning every day means you are not stuck at a certain capacity level; you know more today than you did yesterday, and you can do more tomorrow than you could today.

- **Get into the habit of using the word 'yet' when thinking about what you can or cannot achieve**

I can't pass my driving test **yet**; I can't speak French **yet**; I don't have the experience I need for promotion **yet**. Many people refer to this as having a growth mindset. You can learn new skills and accumulate further information at any age.

- **Be realistic and make decisions based on evidence, not emotion**

Take some time and gather evidence. When faced with a challenge, you may become stressed and make an emotional rather than a rational decision. Mindfulness, see chapter 3, can help you to make better decisions under stress. Gathering evidence means that your choices will be better made and more likely to lead to a successful outcome, which builds self-confidence.

➢ **Focus on your goals, your skills, and your progress, not other people's**

Being competitive can be healthy in the right circumstances, but not if it's damaging your self-confidence. Focus on yourself and what you want to achieve, and measure your progress towards your goals, not someone else's. What matters to you is not the same as what matters to someone else. Their focus will be different from yours, producing different outcomes. People with healthy self-confidence can celebrate other people's success because they have an abundance mindset; there is enough success for everyone, so focus on achieving your own success.

➢ **Invest in your physical well-being**

Physical activity and a healthy diet will make you feel better and more in control of your life. Set physical goals such as walking 5,000 steps daily and use an app on your phone to record and celebrate when you achieve your goal. Undertake mindful activities such as swimming, running, gardening, or walking on a beach. It gives you time to gently let go of the destructive thoughts contributing to low self-confidence. At the same time, you will benefit from the positive emotional impacts of exercise, such as lower levels of the stress hormone cortisol in your bloodstream.

➢Learn from other people's successes and failures

You can learn much from what other people do and their actions' positive or negative outcomes. Observe people who seem to be happy, contented, and achieving their goals in life and try and replicate what they do. When Steven Covey was writing his book, *The Seven Habits of Highly Effective People*, he identified a group of highly successful people. He observed actions that were common to the group and which they constantly practised. You can do the same. Who in your life is succeeding at something you want to achieve? Observe what they do and copy them. You could ask them to be your mentor, so you don't have to repeat all their mistakes. Many people are delighted to mentor others; it makes them feel better about themselves. If you do have a mentor, learn to accept constructive criticism. It's not easy, but it can save you from repeating the same mistakes.

➢Remember when you succeeded previously

> *"If you want confidence, get out there and do something. Achieve. Because nothing can replace the confidence of achievement. When it comes to confidence, achievement is gold, silver, and bronze all rolled into one."– Robert Kelsey*

Success can be contagious: succeeding at one thing will build your confidence that you can succeed at something completely different. When you are trying to complete a couch to 5K, you may remember how you passed your driving test. Remembering how you succeeded in one task helps you to be successful in an unrelated task. The connection between these unrelated tasks is your ability to be successful. When you do have a success, celebrate it. This helps to embed it in your memory, and you will be able to recall it more easily.

- **Don't let the fear of failure or making mistakes stop you from trying**

What are you going to fail better at tomorrow? Challenge yourself and realistically push your boundaries. These can be small challenges that cause some discomfort. For example, make sure you speak at least once in every team meeting if a lack of confidence has inhibited you in the past. But give yourself the time to prepare appropriately for your contribution and remember that you have prepared when it comes time to speak. Don't personalise mistakes: making mistakes does not make you a failure.

- **Pursue big goals and small goals in different parts of your life**

Don't put all your emotional eggs in one basket. Have big and small goals in your personal and work life. Then, if one area of your life becomes difficult, you can still thrive in another part. Often your brain isn't that good at understanding perspective. A small success can feel as joyous as a big success. So set and achieve small goals such as keeping a gratitude diary, walking 5,000 steps, or learning one new Spanish word. And then deliver on your goals. And take time to say well done to yourself. Keep renewing your plans. When you achieve one goal, think of a new one, and continue to challenge yourself.

➢**Don't give up**!

> *"The greatest glory in living lies not in never falling, but in rising every time we fall." – Ralph Waldo Emerson*

If you don't give up, you may fail but you're not a failure. Not everything goes right, but most things improve when you stick to them. How many people sadly give up on the verge of success? Not only have they wasted their effort, but they may have damaged their self-confidence about succeeding in the future.

Self-Confidence Is The Trigger For Action

Society forgives many failures because we all hope to share in the benefits when someone does something innovative. Edison had over a thousand failures but created a working light bulb that benefited everyone.

At the individual level, confidence stimulates action. If your action is successful, it increases your self-confidence. Confidence builds through hard work, risk-taking, success, and even failure. One extract from Samuel Beckett's 1983 story "Worstward Ho" has become a mantra of how to succeed in the hi-tech, high-risk start-ups of Silicon Valley:

"Ever tried, ever failed, no matter, try again, fail again, fail better."

The key to building self-confidence, the key to success? Failing better!

When Professor Zachary Estes of the City University London examined why some students scored poorly in solving puzzles, he found that a significant reason was that they hadn't attempted to answer some of the questions. So, he repeated the experiment, but everyone had to try at least to solve all the puzzles. Scores substantially improved for those who had not previously attempted all the tasks. To succeed, you have to be prepared to fail.[46]Self-confidence enables action, and it is an action that leads to success, even through failure. Success leads to increased self-confidence, more action, more success, and a virtuous, reinforcing cycle.

Measuring Your Self-Confidence

In their book, *The Self-Confidence Workbook: A Guide to Overcoming Self-Doubt and Improving Self-Esteem,,*

Barbara Markway and Celia Ampel include a self-confidence test so that you can get a more objective assessment of how self-confident you are. An article by Barbara Markway includes the test and how to self-score it.[47] See resources at end of the chapter.

The Confidence Gap

The confidence gap is the difference between your actual competence and how you feel about your competence. If your confidence is significantly lower than your competence, it can stop you from achieving your goals in life. Even though you have the talent, knowledge, skills, and commitment to succeed, low self-confidence can brake your progress substantially. It also can hurt your mental health through increased anxiety levels.

The Confidence Gap Impacts More Women Than Men

In 2003, David Dunning, of the Dunning Kruger Effect, joined Joyce Ehrlinger of Washington State University and undertook research into male and female self-confidence and its impact on their behaviour.[48] They asked a group of male and female college science students to rate themselves for scientific ability, complete a scientific test and then predict how well they did. Before completing the quiz, the female students rated their ability as 6.5 out of 10 on average, and the male students gave themselves an average of 7.6. After completing the science test, female students predicted they had got 5.8 out of 10 questions correct, and male students predicted a substantially higher 7.1. And how did they perform? Almost the same: the female students scored 7.5 and the male students 7.9. Before giving the students their scores, they asked them if they wanted to compete in a science competition; only 49 per cent of the female students signed up for the competition, compared with 71 per cent of the male students. The female students felt less confident in their ability, evaluated their performance as lower than they actually achieved, and then were less likely to progress to try to realise a further opportunity. They did this based on their self-confidence, not their actual performance or competence.

Low Self-Confidence In The Workplace

This behaviour continues into people's careers, affecting promotion and salary levels. Women will apply for a job if they meet 90 per cent of the qualifications needed, and men will apply for the same position when they meet 50 per cent of the criteria. Hewlett Packard found that men applied for a promotion when they met 60 per cent of the requirements, and women only applied if they met 100 per cent.[49]Linda Babcock, a professor of economics at Carnegie Mellon University and the author of *Women Don't Ask*, has found that men initiate salary negotiations four times as often as women do and that when women do negotiate, they ask for 30 per cent less money than men do.[50]

Imposter Syndrome

In 1978, psychologists Pauline Clance and Suzanne Imes studied 150 successful women and discovered a psychological condition called Imposter Syndrome. All the women in their study were objectively high achievers, having received formal recognition for their academic and professional successes. [51] Sadly, many did not feel successful because they could not internalise it. They did not believe they were the cause of their success; instead, it was luck or other external circumstances. They felt they shouldn't be in their role because they didn't have everyone else's skills and abilities. Many expressed the constant worry that they would be exposed as a fraud, as an imposter.

Initially, they believed this was a female-only trait but discovered anyone can be affected by imposter syndrome: up to 70 per cent of people experience it during their lifetime, but women and members of minority groups are at a higher risk. If you are one of the only women, people from an ethnic or religious minority or people with a disability in your role or organisation, you are at higher risk of developing imposter syndrome. When you look around, do you see people who look like you? If not, it may make you feel you shouldn't be there. As an individual, you are also at a higher risk of developing imposter syndrome at breakthrough moments in your life – the joy of getting promoted may turn to anxiety about not being good enough in your new role.

Five Signs That You May Be Suffering From Imposter Syndrome

One: You believe your success is unearned

You explain your success through luck or circumstance. You don't deserve it; it's due to external events.

Two: You are a procrastinator

You delay starting to do something to avoid the chance that you will fail and be exposed for the fraud you are. You delay starting a project, you delay finishing a project, and you delay submitting a project. Great video by Keith Urban – see resources section at end of the chapter.

Three: You are a perfectionist

Your work is never good enough, so you don't know when to stop. You spend an hour over a two-line email. You can't avoid being in early and leaving late even though it negatively affects other parts of your life. You think achieving 98 per cent in a test is a failure and may struggle to be genuinely happy for other people when they succeed. We discuss perfectionism below.

Four: You are afraid of failure and exposure

No matter how often you check, you still think there is the potential for a significant error in your work. You are highly vigilant about potential disasters when you go to work each morning. This triggers anxiety, stress, and even obsessional behaviours to try and keep control.

Five: You need to be the best just to be ok

Setting the bar so high that being successful gives next to no satisfaction – being brilliant is just the baseline. Seeking exceptional people to compare yourself with, not to copy but to show how you aren't good enough.

How To Reduce The Impact Of Imposter Syndrome

Measure yourself on the Clance IP Scale

Find out if you are being affected by imposter syndrome. You can download the Clance IP Scale, see the resources at end of the chapter. An objective assessment will help you know how much of a problem you face. If you score highly, consider therapy, and use the therapist as a coach.

Identify and label the feelings you are having

Mindfulness meditation can help. Practise identifying and labelling the thoughts you are having. Disassociate from these thoughts by saying to yourself, "I note that I am identifying this thought as a negative thought". Accepting that many people have the same negative thoughts can help to neutralise the "What's wrong with me?" feeling.

Gather evidence about your competence

It's easy to over-focus on what you don't have and what you can't do. Gathering objective evidence helps you to move towards appraisal. You may find that an honest assessment of your competence identifies areas where you genuinely need to improve – imposter syndrome throws a blanket of confusion over your strengths and weaknesses.

Are you really an imposter?

What are your values? Do you value honesty? Do you live by your values? If so, how could you be an imposter, a fraudster? Self-confidence and self-esteem do overlap. Improving your self-esteem and how you value yourself can improve your self-confidence, as discussed in the next chapter.

Have open conversations with mentors whom you trust and admire

If possible, talk to someone who has experienced imposter syndrome. As stated above, up to 70 per cent of people sometimes suffer from imposter syndrome. It often helps to talk to someone who has experienced what you are facing. Evidence suggests that talking to someone who 'knows' is beneficial, not just for imposter syndrome but also for depression, anxiety, and physical health issues. They also found evidence that both parties benefit and acting as a mentor or listening ear reduces the chance of the problem returning.

Perfectionism

There are two types of perfectionism, adaptive and maladaptive.

Adaptive perfectionism contributes to your mental health, as you are investing in becoming the most competent version of yourself. The ancient Greeks termed it eudaemonic well-being, and we are still using the term. You set challenging but realistic targets for yourself and often achieve them. When you don't achieve them, you try again or adjust your targets.

Maladaptive perfectionism stops you from becoming the best version of yourself because you set unrealistic targets that lead to constant failures. And if you do achieve these unrealistic targets, it doesn't help: you instantly go into a spiral of dismissing the targets as being flawed, and that's the only reason you were able to achieve them. You are likely to avoid tasks where there is a risk of failure and spend excessive time trying to make mundane tasks perfect.

Maladaptive perfectionism in itself is not a diagnosable mental disorder but it usually coexists with various forms of anxiety including behaviours such as OCD. Cognitive behaviour therapy can be very effective in changing behaviours such as perfectionism and imposter syndrome. In the resources section below there are links that will provide more detailed information re perfectionism.

Summary

- Self-confidence is a significant element of your mental health.

- It is not static; you can become more self-confident.

- Healthy self-confidence supports your physical well-being.

- You can take action every day that will lead to more healthy self-confidence.

- Imposter syndrome is caused by the confidence gap, and low self-confidence in highly successful people.

- You can often reduce the impact of imposter syndrome by challenging your thought patterns using mindfulness meditation and talking to a mentor or someone who has experienced it themselves.

Resources

- Measure your self-confidence:https://www.psychologytoday.com/intl/blog/shyness-is-nice/201812/5-reasons-people-have-low-self-confidence

- You can download the Clance IP Scale at: https://www.paulineroseclance.com/pdf/IPTestandscoring.pdf.

➢Excellent 21-minute TEDx Talk video on what imposter syndrome feels like and what to do about it: Lou Solomon, "The surprising solution to the imposter syndrome" https://www.youtube.com/watch?v=whyUPLJZljE

➢A really good 4-minute video explaining why perfectionism may become a problem and a structured approach to reducing its impact. "How to recognise and cure perfectionism" https://www.youtube.com/watch?v=zTj25XawoDk

➢You can measure your Perfectionism using The Almost Perfect Scale: https://heartofsubstance.com/wp-content/uploads/2020/02/Almost-Perfect-Scale_updatedversion.pdf

➢Very valuable video by psychotherapist Mark Tyrrel talking about how he helped a patient affected by perfectionism: https://www.youtube.com/watch?v=T1bg7I2bXBU

➢Great video by Tim Urban about procrastination, "Inside the mind of the master procrastinator": https://www.youtube.com/watch?v=arj7oStGLkU

Next Chapter

In the next chapter, we will look at how to achieve healthy self-esteem. This is your assessment of the value of the life you are living. Self-confidence and self-esteem are separate but overlapping sources of mental health.

CHAPTER 6: HEALTHY SELF-ESTEEM

"Low self-esteem is like driving through life with your hand-brake on." – Maxwell Maltz

Healthy self-esteem, believing you are a good person, a person of value, is central to your mental health. There are times in your life, in everyone's life, when events and people's behaviour will challenge your self-esteem and mental health. Healthy self-esteem can help you to navigate challenging times in your life. Sadly, unhealthy self-esteem tends to bring more difficult times into our lives, including depression, anxiety, stress, relationship problems, performance issues, addictions, and risk-taking behaviour.

What It Feels Like To Have Healthy Self-Esteem

➢ **You believe you are a good, worthy, and lovable person even when life gets difficult**
Healthy self-esteem is not brittle, it's resilient. You feel positive about yourself even through challenging times in your life. You face difficulties and failures but you still believe you are a person of value.

➢ **You feel that you deserve the love and respect you receive from other people**
You are not an imposter; you believe you are a genuinely good person, a kind person who does good things and makes the world a better place for those close to you.

➢ **You value yourself as you are now, not for what you will be in the future**
Your self-worth isn't in the future. It's here and now. You're a good person deserving of happiness now. You feel you can become a better person, but you are a good person already.

- **You have positive self-talk and treat yourself with care, kindness, and respect**
  You say things to yourself that you would say to someone you liked. The little voice in your head is a positive, kind, empathetic, and forgiving voice.

- **You believe in your potential to grow, learn, change, and improve**
  You're not yet your best self. You can grow as a person and do greater things. You are motivated to become a better person.

- **You have flaws and make mistakes, but they don't threaten your identity or worth**
  No one is perfect, you have failures and make bad decisions, but you are still a good person trying your best and learning from your mistakes.

Building Your Self-Esteem

"No one can make you feel inferior without your consent." – Eleanor Roosevelt

Some of your self-esteem is linked to genetics, but identical twins do not have identical self-esteem. There are many contributors to your self-esteem besides your genetic makeup, including the parenting skills you experienced, your successes and failures in life, decisions you have made, and even random events over which you had no control. Researchers have been able to identify actions that you can take to build healthy self-esteem.

1. Live your life mindfully.

Researchers in Australia found a direct connection between practising mindfulness and increased self-esteem.[52] They found that even fifteen minutes a day of mindfulness meditation increased self-esteem. Mindfulness increases self-compassion, positive emotions, and acceptance, all of which contribute to how you feel about yourself. Practising mindfulness also helps you to be aware of your thoughts and emotions, including negative self-talk, which can destroy self-esteem. When you practise mindfulness, you learn to identify the critical internal voice saying you are not good enough. By practising mindfulness, you can neutralise the voice, taking away its power. There are many online mindfulness resources; many provide meditations for free.

2. Be honest with yourself.

Look in the mirror and be honest about what you see. Honest about both your good points and your bad points. This can be difficult, maybe even painful. We have all made mistakes in the past and will all do so again in the future. No one is perfect, so do not set yourself up for failure. Think about the good things you have done in your life, the times you have been kind and compassionate. Do more good things and actions you are proud of, and your self-esteem will grow. If you feel guilty about things you have done in the past, consider the process of self-forgiveness discussed in chapter 2. The gateway to self-forgiveness is being able to say honestly that you would not do the same thing now. Forgive your younger self, atone for what you have done, learn from it, and become a better person.

3. It's your life; take ownership.

I was delivering a mental health training programme for police officers in Belfast. I was discussing factors that contribute to the increased incidence of mental illnesses in the police compared to the general public. One of the factors is that police officers are roughly twice as likely to use alcohol dangerously compared to the general public. Often this behaviour is linked to trying to cope with the high levels of stress and trauma they are exposed to. One officer spoke about their struggles with alcohol, saying the day they stopped abusing alcohol was the day they stopped blaming other people for their problems. Are you exercising? Are you eating healthily? Are you getting a good night's sleep? You're in charge of your own choices and actions. It will hurt your self-esteem if you blame others for your own decisions. It is also not healthy to expect others to make us happy. Hold yourself accountable for your words and actions rather than blaming others or making excuses. Take responsibility for your successes and failures: bad things happen to everyone; what is important is how we respond to failures (see chapter 9 on emotional resilience). Learn from your mistakes, grow as a person, and develop higher levels of self-esteem. If your problems are beyond your capacity to resolve on your own, access help such as talking to your doctor or engaging in talking therapy.

4. Don't be invisible, be yourself.

Even though you may want to speak at a work meeting because you have something valuable to contribute, there may be barriers that stop you from doing so. Two of the most common obstacles that make us invisible are low self-confidence and low self-esteem. Low self-confidence (chapter 5) is when you believe you are not competent enough to contribute even though you are as competent as everyone else. Low self-esteem stops you from contributing because you don't feel good enough. Knowing and living your values and, when appropriate, respectfully expressing them is being assertive. Not living your values or not expressing them often leads to resentment, disappointment, and lower self-esteem. Tackling the negative self-talk associated with low self-esteem, see below, will make it easier for you to contribute to the group. Being assertive does not mean being obnoxious or inappropriately aggressive. It does not mean upholding your rights whilst dismissing everyone else's.

5. Have a purpose in your life.

Imagine you have lived to the ripe old age of 100 and are reflecting on your life that has hopefully been well-lived. You may be proud of many things in your life, your family, your friends, your career, the obstacles you have overcome, and the successes you have achieved. Many things in your life will have been unplanned but others will have been planned – you will have set goals, taken actions to achieve your goals, and overcome barriers to succeed. Living purposely is this more planned area of your life.

Many people find purpose in their job or career. People become teachers, first responders, nurses, and pursue other careers because they are driven to help others. Others start businesses because of the challenges and rewards that they often want to hand on to their children. Many find purpose in raising and supporting a family. For others, religious beliefs or politics play a central role in their lives. Your purpose may not be as clear as you would wish. If you are struggling to find meaning in your life, you usually will not go wrong in seeking to be of value to others. Volunteering is a very positive step towards finding your purpose and will help build healthy self-esteem.

6. Live your life according to what you believe is right.

"Do what you feel in your heart to be right – for you'll be criticised anyway. You'll be damned if you do and damned if you don't." – Eleanor

Roosevelt

What is important to you in life? Do you have rules or values that inform the decisions you make? You may have values similar to these:

> Compassion: I am kind and caring to everyone I engage with.
> Accountability: I am responsible for my words, actions, and results.
> Respect: I value everyone and treat people with dignity and empathy.
> Integrity: I build trust through responsible actions and honest relationships.
> Teamwork: I achieve more when I collaborate and work with others.

Values are statements to aspire to, but they are also decision-making tools. They tell you what to do so that you are living a life of your values, not someone else's. There is often a short-term cost to living your values because you choose to do the right thing rather than the convenient thing. Few core values are fundamentally self-serving; far more often, they cause you to put other people's benefit before your own self-interest.

Negative Self-Talk Damages Your Self-Esteem.

Guilt and shame are examples of negative self-talk; both damage your self-esteem but the impact of both can be reduced. Guilt is negative self-talk that tells you that you have done something wrong; shame is negative self-talk that tells you that something is wrong with you.

Guilt

Guilt is a voice telling you that you have done something bad. Feeling guilty is a sign of empathy; you realise that your actions have hurt yourself or someone else. In chapter 2, we looked at forgiveness, including self-forgiveness. This was achieved through a four-step process: accept responsibility; allow yourself to feel guilt or remorse as a step to change; if it's possible, try to make amends with whomever you've hurt, and if you can't, then atone by undertaking a positive action such as volunteering, donating, or an act of kindness; and learn from the experience and grow as a person.

Everyone makes mistakes and has things for which they feel regretful. Forgiving yourself often requires finding a way to learn from the experience and grow as a person. Here is a quote I use every time I feel guilty about something I have done.

> *"I shouldn't have known better because I couldn't have known better because I hadn't yet learnt what I know now. Today I forgive my younger self." – Sandy Newbigging*

If you can say honestly, "I wouldn't do the same thing now," it allows you to go through self-forgiveness, become a better person, and move on.

Shame

Shame is a powerful emotion that can cause you to feel that there is something wrong with you. That you are outside what is acceptable in a person, that you're worthless, and that you can't change. Shame often develops when other people constantly tell you you're not good enough or treat you poorly, especially when you are young, turning that treatment into a belief about yourself. Shame can start because of how a parent might speak to you when you did something they considered wrong or disappointing. For example, if you wet the bed, were you told that it was all right and little fuss made or did they say something such as "Why do you always do this? What's wrong with you?" This negative external voice with repetition can trigger a similar internal voice saying the same thing – there is something wrong with you; you're not as good as everyone else.

If your feelings of shame or guilt significantly affect your self-esteem, learn to challenge them. Practising mindfulness meditation is excellent in helping you identify and understand your thoughts and your self-talk. Mindfulness is the practical application of metacognition, your ability to think about your thoughts even as you have them. By practising mindfulness meditation, you can identify and label the destructive thoughts that make up your negative self-talk. You will often start to observe that the statements are extreme, unfair, unjustified, and without evidence. You would never say something as hurtful to someone else you liked.

When you can identify and label your negative self-talk, you can challenge what the statements are saying – what is the evidence that these statements are factual? Use the triple-column technique to reframe your negative self-talk. Identify a negative statement, collect the evidence, and remove its power by reframing it into positive self-talk.

Negative self-talk: I never do anything right

Evidence: I do lots of things well, I do my best, and I'm conscientious and reliable.

Positive self-talk: I am a competent person with the skills needed to do my job, and I am prepared to learn and grow.

Be kinder to yourself. Everyone has flaws and makes

mistakes. Even if your mistakes seem huge, accept that you're only human. Learn from the past, but don't get stuck in it. Practise self-compassion; see chapter 7. Be quicker to ask for help. Be the first in the queue for help; it builds your resilience and ability to bounce back and continue after setbacks in life. A support network can give you an outlet to talk things out when necessary and boost your sense of belonging. Asking for help can make you feel better even before you get the help.

In her TEDx talk, "Meet yourself: A user's guide to building self-esteem", Niko Everett explains how she built her own self-esteem whilst supporting a group of girls as they build theirs. It is a very personal and moving description of how so many people can hardly say one positive thing about themselves, and she gives great practical advice:

➢Spend more time with people who make you feel good.

➢Turn up the volume on positive thoughts and delete the negative ones.

➢Start telling the people around you what you like about them and help to jump-start their positive thinking.

➢When you receive a compliment, look the person

in the eye and say thank you.

The link to her TEDx talk is in the resources at the end of the chapter.

Don't Cheerlead Your Own Critics

In April 1910, Teddy Roosevelt made a speech in Paris known as the "Man in The Arena" Speech.[53]

"It is not the critic who counts; not the man who points out how the strong man stumbles or where the doer of deeds could have done them better. The credit belongs to the man who is actually in the arena, whose face is marred by dust and sweat and blood; who strives valiantly; who errs, who comes short again and again because there is no effort without error and shortcoming; but who does actually strive to do the deeds; who knows great enthusiasms, the great devotions; who spends himself in a worthy cause; who at the best knows, in the end, the triumph of high achievement, and who at the worst, if he fails, at least fails while daring greatly, so that his place shall never be with those cold and timid souls who neither know victory nor defeat."

Imagine you are in the arena, look up at the emperor's box and see your main critics; see them pointing out all your mistakes, your failures, your shaming secrets. Notice who is sitting in the emperor's chair: is it you? Often, you are your harshest critic, your negative self-talk constantly repeating what others have said to you in the past. Cognitive behaviour therapy, or other talking therapy, can help you challenge these feelings.

Consider talking to someone who has experienced similar feelings. If you cannot do it on your own, seek help; seeking help in itself is empowering.

Summary

- Healthy self-esteem helps you to achieve mental health.
- Low self-esteem is associated with the most common mental health issues and destructive behaviours.
- You can improve your self-esteem: it's not fixed. Try the six steps described above.
- Guilt tells you that you are a good person who has done something wrong. Try self-forgiveness as described in chapter 2; if that doesn't work, consider asking for help.
- Shame is telling you that you are a terrible person. If you can, change how you feel but if you can't do it on your own, seek someone to help you.
- Don't be your worst critic: others will happily play that role without invitation.
- Learn to be kind to yourself, speak to yourself as you would to a good friend. Practise self-compassion.

Resources

➢ Very powerful TEDx talk by Niko Everett about her practical experience of helping a group of girls, and herself, build self-esteem. "Meet yourself: a user's guide to building self-esteem": https://www.youtube.com/watch?v=uOrzmFUJtrs

- ➢Three excellent videos by Dr Brene Brown talking about vulnerability, shame and perfectionism:
  https://www.youtube.com/watch?v=iCvmsMzlF7o
  https://www.youtube.com/watch?v=psN1DORYY0
  https://www.youtube.com/watch?v=MF8gTBGDMN8

- ➢You can measure your self-esteem online using the Rosenberg Self-Esteem Scale at:
  https://wwnorton.com/college/psych/psychsci/media/rosenberg.htm#:~:text=The%20scale%20ranges%20from%200,15%20suggest%20low%20self%2Desteem

Next Chapter

Being compassionate is great for your mental health and the benefit of the people you help. You can learn to become more compassionate and competent in your approach to helping others. Self-compassion is also a material contributor to your mental health.

CHAPTER 7: BEING COMPASSIONATE

"If you want others to be happy, practise compassion. If you want to be happy, practise compassion." – The Dalai Lama

Compassion and kindness are hardwired in our genes. An infant can show compassion before they are old enough to have learned to be compassionate.[54] Toddlers have been observed comforting their distressed playmates and being happier when they give treats to their friends than when receiving treats themselves. Think of evolution and it makes sense. Humans survive best in groups. The group can protect you from dangerous predators, humans, or animals, and the group members can co-operate to provide, store, and cook food. Helping others in your family, tribe, village, or community is not necessarily a selfless act. You need individuals in your group to be strong so that your group is strong. They can then support or protect you in turn as a member of the group.

Compassion, however, can be completely selfless. It is an act of kindness triggered by another person's pain, not self-interest. There is a charity in the UK called Cherished Gowns. People send their wedding dresses to this small charity, and their volunteers cut the wedding dresses up and make them into babies' gowns. The gowns, accompanied by a hat, pair of booties, a blanket, and a cloth nappy, are then given to the bereaved parents of children who are stillborn, miscarried, or die shortly after birth so the babies can be dressed for their burials. The waiting list to donate wedding dresses is currently closed at 1000.

Benefits To You Of Being Compassionate

> *"That is what compassion does. It challenges our assumptions, our sense of self-limitation, our worthlessness, of not having a place in the world." – Sharon Salzburg*

Research shows that being compassionate, whilst selfless, is as good for you as it is for the person you're helping. Specific benefits that researchers have found include:

- ➢The more compassion you show, the more happiness you feel, and the less you experience depression.[55]

- ➢Being more compassionate builds social connections.[56] When you help someone, even a stranger, you trigger the production of the bonding hormone oxytocin, which makes you feel connected.

- ➢Compassion reduces stress.[57] The production of cortisol, the stress hormone, is reduced by soothing ourselves. Compassion, including self-compassion, is part of our soothing response.

- ➢Being more compassionate helps to improve parent

and child relationships.[58]

➢ Compassion for colleagues is linked to increased job satisfaction.[59]

The Difference Between Compassion, Sympathy, And Empathy

If you are sympathetic to someone, you recognise that they are in pain. If a colleague is grieving because a parent died, you understand they are in pain. You may never have suffered the bereavement of a parent, but you can understand it must be painful. You have sympathy **for** someone.

If you are empathetic to someone, you are close enough to feel their pain. You can feel your colleague's pain because you remember what it was like when you lost your parent last year. Or you take the time to stand in their shoes and experience what they are feeling. You cannot take away their pain, but you can take the time to listen to them so they know you care. You feel empathy **with** someone.

When you are compassionate, you understand and even share someone's pain and are motivated to take action to reduce their pain. A relative suffers an injury and is housebound. You feel sympathetic for their plight so you call round and visit them with a bunch of flowers. By listening to their explanation of what day-to-day life is like for them, you develop a more complete understanding of how difficult things are; you empathise with them. You volunteer to shop for them. You call in every evening to cook meals because you do not want them to suffer unnecessarily. You are compassionate **to** someone.

Becoming More Compassionate

> *"Compassion is the wish to see others free from suffering." – The Dalai Lama*

Given that being compassionate towards ourselves and others is so helpful for our mental health, how can we become more compassionate?

Step 1: Become More Aware Of Other People's Distress

Compassion is triggered by the initial observation of pain or distress in another person. You will not become compassionate if no one is suffering or upset. You can become more observant of other people's distress by becoming more mindful, not moving through life on automatic pilot. You can also learn to be more aware of people's signs when distressed (see the Look Listen Link model below).

Step 2: Develop A Sympathetic Response

Before you become motivated to help someone, you need to have sympathy for that person. You may not know precisely what is happening but you are aware that the person is distressed. If you are indifferent to the person, you will not feel sympathy for them and will not try to help them.

Step 3: Empathy

If you feel sympathy for the person, you can become motivated to find out more. Empathetic listening can help you to understand what is happening to them and how distressed they are. Empathy is listening without trying to solve another person's problem. Sometimes all that can be achieved, or all that is needed is to listen (see the Look Listen Link model below).

Dr Helen Riess, Associate Professor of Psychiatry at Harvard Medical School, explains the power of empathy in her video, see resources at end of the chapter. She also has an acronym which explains how you can become more empathetic:

E – Eye contact. People need to feel they are being seen: this originates with the mother-baby bond. If you want to build a connection with someone, eye contact is usually needed.

M – Muscles in your face. Your facial expression either builds empathy or destroys it. If you are irritated it shows, if you are bored or distracted it shows in your face. If you're genuinely interested that shows, too.

P – Posture. Is your posture open or closed? A closed posture is a barrier to empathy and connection.

A – Affect. Listen to the emotions that someone is

telling you. Most people give lots of clues to what they are feeling if you actively listen to them.

T – Tone of voice. Your tone of voice can express emotions that are unsaid. You can pick up someone's irritation, excitement, or distress in their tone of voice even if the content of what they are saying does not disclose anything.

H – Hear the whole person. You don't know everything that is going on in someone's life so giving advice or solutions often isn't that useful. Listening to the person and trying to understand their worldview without the need to judge or advise will often lead to a more positive outcome.

Y – Your response. We can actually physically feel other people's pain. fMRI scans showed people's responses to mild electric shocks were very similar to the response when they didn't receive shocks but were told that their partner was receiving the shocks. Empathy is about shared feelings.

Step 4: Look, Listen, Link: A Model To Competently And Safely Help Someone

So, what can you do when you see that someone's distressed? This model can give you a safe and effective structure to follow. The Look, Listen, Link model was developed for use in schools in the State of Washington. It provides an effective, safe, and structured way to help another person. It has been evaluated as being an effective and safe model to use if you want to provide help to someone who may be distressed. Safe for them, and also safe for you.

- **Look**

The first step in the model is for you to identify signs that someone may be distressed. Not everyone gives clear signs that they are upset, and some people will try to hide their distress. This can make it difficult to know if you should offer help. Maybe you are mistaken, and it will be embarrassing if you offer help that isn't needed or appreciated.For this reason, the Look Listen Link model is a three-step model: signs are just signs, and sometimes the signs may be wrong. The second step is to ask questions which will help you understand more clearly what is happening. Step one, however, is critical: if you don't notice any signs of distress, you will not be concerned. Signs may be verbal or non-verbal. Verbal signs include someone saying they are distressed. What you should try to avoid doing is giving unrealistic reassurances that everything is going to be all right. To someone distressed, it can sound like you are contradicting or dismissing their concerns. It is unlikely to make them feel better. Allowing someone to talk is positive for them, but also for you. You can develop a fuller understanding of the situation through listening. Signs of distress can include:

- Aggression
- Substance abuse

- Hurting themselves
- Acting recklessly
- Disengaging from family activities
- Becoming more placid than usual
- Becoming more angry than usual
- Being visibly upset.

Signs may or may not be valid but noticing signs of distress is the first step. You can then move on to step 2 and develop a better understanding of the situation through asking questions and listening to the answers.

- **Listen**

> *"When people talk, listen completely. Most people never listen." – Ernest Hemingway*

Broadly there are two ways to listen to someone – selective and active. Selective listening is what we usually do by default. It takes far less concentration or effort than active listening. We half-listen to someone whilst looking at our phones. Or we simply hope they will finish talking and let us get back to what we have to do. Selective listening often gets us through the day without being exhausted, but often it is not helpful. It can cause us to miss what someone is trying to say to us.

Active listening is when you pay attention to someone and focus on what they are saying – listening to the actual words they are using and asking them questions about what they have said to find out more. Instead of guessing what somebody is trying to tell us, you can become an effective listener by linking your questions to the other person's answers. For example, you're worried about a friend. You ask them, "How are you getting on?" They reply that they are having a bit of a bad time. Don't guess. Ask, "What do you mean by a bad time?" "I have a problem at work". "What's the problem at work?"

You become an effective listener by listening to your friend's words and linking your questions to what they said. You will better understand what is happening in your friend's life and how upset or distressed they are. There is also another significant benefit. Helping your friend to talk about their issues is a positive thing. When people talk to someone else about their distress, it can help them to identify their feelings and can help reduce stress. People also tend to feel more motivated to engage with help if they have talked to another person about what is upsetting them. You do not need answers at this stage; what is valuable is that you have listened, and your friend has been heard.

➢ Link

The third step is to Link. You may have assumed that if someone needs help, they will ask for it. Very often, this isn't what happens. I recently delivered two training workshops in a single week to two very different audiences. The first group were police officers in London attending suicide prevention skills training. I provide this programme every month, and I always ask the group why a colleague of theirs, if distressed, might not ask for help. The answers are always similar. Their colleague would be too embarrassed to ask for help and too frightened of the potential impact on their career. They would be too ashamed to tell anyone how bad they felt. And they would be concerned that their fellow officers would judge them as weak and possibly reject them from the team. The second programme was for a group of about 60 twelve-year-olds in a school in a small market town in County Down. The workshop I was delivering focused on how to become more emotionally resilient. I asked the twelve-year-olds why their friend might not ask for help if they were upset. The answers were that their friend would be too ashamed, frightened, and embarrassed to ask. And they thought their friends wouldn't want to be their friends any more.

It doesn't matter how old you are or your role in life;

you could find it difficult or impossible to ask for help. It is estimated that about three out of four people in distress cannot access help. Being compassionate may include providing the support that the person needs, but often it is far safer and more effective for you to link them to the help they need but can't ask for. Maybe your friend needs to see a medical practitioner and get a proper assessment. Perhaps they need to get legal advice. Maybe they need a therapist to listen to them and understand what they are going through. You can act as a bridge to the help they need, making all the difference. Help them to make the appointment, go with them if you can, or follow up and make sure they went.

Compassion Fatigue

Because of your role in life, you may be exposed to a level of other people's suffering that causes you to become stressed and even traumatised. For example, first responders, therapists, caring professionals, and members of the medical and veterinary professions are all at risk of developing compassion fatigue. Compassion fatigue can cause you to feel exhausted physically and emotionally and trigger negative feelings about yourself because you do not think you can care the way you should. Compassion fatigue can be secondary trauma and, if not addressed, may develop into a diagnosable disorder such as PTSD or clinical depression. Addressing compassion fatigue usually means:

➢Stepping back from the source of your distress, which might mean taking time off work or caring responsibilities.

➢Ensuring you have practical barriers between work and private life.

➢ Considering talking therapies.

➢Accessing peer support, particularly a peer who has suffered compassion fatigue.

➢Practising self-compassion.

Self-Compassion

> *"Talk to yourself as you would to someone you love." – Dr Brené Brown*

Sometimes the person in pain is you. Self-compassion entails being kind to yourself when you are in pain or life has turned negative. Self-compassion means you don't ignore your distress or hurt yourself further with self-criticism. Instead, you recognise that this is a difficult time and ask, "How can I care for and comfort myself at this moment?"

Benefits Of Self-Compassion

Researchers have found substantial benefits of self-compassion, including:

➢Lower levels of stress
Self-compassion reduces stress due to self-kindness, and more positive self-talk.[60] Compassion soothes you and reduces your stress response. Self-compassion helps to reduce PTSD.[61]

➢Improved mental health
Self-compassion is related to increased well-being.[62] Increased levels of oxytocin and reduced cortisol

levels contribute to your good mental health.

➢**Lower levels of anxiety and increased psychological well-being**[63]

Anxiety can significantly damage your mental health and, if untreated, often develops into depression. Self-compassion reduces anxiety levels by soothing our stress response.

➢**Reduced burn-out among care providers**.[64]

Many people working to provide care to others are at risk of compassion fatigue if they don't practise self-care and compassion.

Three Elements Of Self-Compassion

The leading researcher on self-compassion, Dr Kristin Neff of the University of Texas, has identified self-compassion as having three elements:

1. **Showing yourself self-kindness instead of self-judgement**.

Be kind towards yourself when stressed or upset, rather than ignoring your feelings or criticising yourself for feeling that way. Treat yourself as you would a friend who is stressed and reduce the pressure on yourself if you can.

2. **Recognising your common humanity instead of suffering in isolation.**

Accept that you are the same as everyone else.

Sometimes you are hurt, sometimes you make mistakes, and sometimes you do things you regret. It's being human. Others in your life are likely to have gone through similar times and sharing your problem with people you trust can be beneficial.

3. **Being mindful of your distress rather than being owned by it.**

Being mindful means being aware of your thoughts and emotions, not suppressing them but also not being owned by them. Avoid labelling yourself as a loser or a failure. Mindfulness meditation reduces stress and builds emotional resilience.

Barriers To Self-Compassion

Given that self-compassion is such a good idea, why do we find it so hard to implement?

➢Evolution

Human beings have developed a negative bias. You react more often, quickly, and intensely to threats than opportunities. You react through your stress response. Self-compassion is the opposite of the stress response. It reduces the level of cortisol and adrenaline in your bloodstream. It may feel as if you aren't vigilant enough for the threats that might be there. It feels like you are letting your defences down; for some people, that is difficult.

➢Stoics

One of the barriers to self-compassion is how some people label it – self-serving, self-indulgent, self-centred, self-pitying, or just straightforward selfish. This negative perception of self-compassion can be traced back to the Stoics of Ancient Greece. They dismissed investing in your own positive emotions as hedonistic and the behaviour of weak, self-indulgent people. Their philosophy was that you should be indifferent to your feelings, positive or negative, and just get on with things. They still have many followers: keep a stiff upper lip and everything will be fine. Sadly, it was a dreadful strategy 2,500 years ago, and it still is. Bottling up your negative emotions is likely to lead to more intense distress and will have a detrimental effect on your mental health.

➢Family background

Early life experiences. Growing up, you may not have been shown how to be compassionate to yourself, and it might never have occurred to you that treating yourself kindly was an option! Some families brush everything under the carpet rather than recognise something is amiss. Sadly, this behaviour will often be learnt by the next generation, but you can take steps to become more self-compassionate.

➢The belief that success will make you happy

When you were at school, your teachers unwittingly sold you a false contract. Study hard, pass your exams, follow a good career, become successful, and you will then be happy. The evidence suggests that often it is precisely the reverse: happy people become more successful. As John Lennon told his teacher, what he wanted to be when he grew up was to be happy, the success would come after. Many successful people are simply not happy. Because of this false contract, they believe that it's their fault. They aren't happy because they aren't working hard enough or haven't achieved enough success yet.

➢**The belief that self-criticism is motivating**

You may believe self-compassion makes you complacent and could undermine your commitment to correcting mistakes. Researchers, however, have found evidence of the exact opposite. Responding with self-compassion subsequently motivates people to improve themselves and their performance.[65] Beating yourself up just makes you feel worse.

Becoming More Self-Compassionate

Dr Neff has developed the self-compassion scale, which may help you to identify how self-compassionate you are.[66] You can complete it at www.self-compassion.org.

The scale measures three pairs of conflicting behaviours related to self-compassion:

- Do you exercise self-kindness, or are you more likely to self-judge and self-criticise?
- Do you recognise that everyone faces problems in their life, or do you feel isolated, that you are the only person suffering on your own?
- Are you mindful of your thoughts and feelings but not owned by them, or do you over-identify and become possessed by your emotions?

Practices that you can incorporate into your daily life include:

- **Practise mindfulness meditation**

Mindfulness meditation will transform how you talk to yourself. Focusing on your breathing allows you to observe your thoughts and emotions, and with practice, you will be able to observe them without emotion or ownership. You can learn to detach from the self-destructive beliefs and statements you are making to yourself. You can learn to disempower these destructive thoughts, and often they will go away.

➢Practise self-forgiveness

Everyone makes mistakes, says nasty things, and doesn't live up to the standards they set for themselves. Everyone, including you. No one is near perfect, and there's no value in pretending you are and punishing yourself. Accept that you have done wrong, feel guilty, make amends or atone, and become a better person. If you can genuinely say you wouldn't do it now, you deserve to forgive your younger self. See the four-step self-forgiveness model in chapter 2.

➢Practise gratitude

It may seem strange to advise you to become more grateful when you don't see lots for which to be thankful. Practising gratitude and keeping a gratitude diary change the way your brain evaluates your life. Without changing anything else, practising gratitude will increase your positive emotions and reduce your depressive and anxious thoughts – which often trigger self-criticism.

➢Talk things over with someone you trust

When you are bottling things up, stressing yourself with destructive self-criticism, you can also catastrophise – every time you think about the things that are upsetting you, you exaggerate how bad things are. Talking aloud to another person can help bring objectivity to how you see things.

➢Optimistically reframe your problem

Optimists explain problems in their lives to themselves differently from pessimists. The optimist identifies the problem as something that will pass, that the problem is limited and specific and that it doesn't make them a bad person. See chapter 4.

➢Take time out

Taking time to soothe yourself is likely to be time well spent. If you can remove yourself from the source of your stress, the level of cortisol and adrenaline in your bloodstream will start to fall. You will feel less under threat and can begin to think more rationally about your situation.

Summary

➢Being compassionate is good for you as well as the person you help.

➢You can become more compassionate: identify distress, develop sympathy, be empathetic and help.

➢The Look Listen Link model is a practical, proven model to use.

➢Self-compassion is as essential as compassion.

➢Self-criticism is not motivating; it is destructive and can trigger depression.

Resources

➢Excellent 17-minute TEDx talk by Dr Helen Riess, Associate Professor Harvard Medical School: "The power of empathy", https://www.youtube.com/watch?v=baHrcC8B4WM

➢Short cartoon video explaining 'Where does compassion really come from?' by Sharon Salzberg. (3 minutes): https://www.youtube.com/watch?v=A4a66aFaIME

➢Dr Kristen Neff's Self-Compassion Scale: https://self-compassion.org/wptest/wp-content/uploads/Self_Compassion_Scale_for_researchers.pdf

➢ Watch Dr Neff explaining the three components of self-compassion (6 mins): https://www.youtube.com/watch?v=11U0h0DPu7k

➢ Series of self-compassion workbooks developed by the Government of Western Australia: https://www.cci.health.wa.gov.au/Resources/Looking-After-Yourself/Self-Compassion

Next Chapter

Loneliness and isolation are detrimental to your mental health. Connecting to other people, friends, family, and community is the key to living a long, happy, and healthy life.

CHAPTER 8: BEING CONNECTED

"There isn't time, so brief is life, for bickerings, apologies, heartburnings, callings to account. There is only time for loving, and but an instant, so to speak, for that." – Mark Twain

Being lonely is being human. Imagine you get your dream job, studying climate change for six months in the Antarctic. You are miles from anywhere but doing something of such value, you are delighted. The spartan living conditions, the constant snow, and other hardships are part of the job. Then before you know it, it's Christmas Day. Now for the first time, you are aware you are on your own, really on your own. You feel lonely because you can't be with your family and friends. You want to be at home being part of the season's celebrations. That's social isolation. Now imagine you are in the Antarctic at Christmas, and you have no one to miss. You have no one you feel you should be with. That's social disconnection. Feelings of loneliness can be caused by social isolation, social disconnection, or both.

Researchers have talked about an epidemic of loneliness in modern times. The number of single-person households has exploded, and the percentage of adults stating they are lonely has doubled from about 20 per cent to 40 per cent.[68] We struggle badly when we feel we are on our own. Feeling lonely is dangerous. Being lonely is a more accurate predictor of death than being obese or smoking a packet of cigarettes a day.

Why Have Human Beings Developed The Ability To Feel Lonely?

If you are thirsty, your body is warning you that you are in danger of becoming dehydrated. If you are hungry, your body is warning you that you may be at risk of starvation. Pain is warning you about a physical disease or injury. Stress is a warning that you could be in danger. Loneliness is warning you that you are becoming disconnected from your 'group', and this was a very dangerous thing during human evolution. Humans have survived living in caves, villages, walled towns, even nomadic tribes. But primarily, humans have survived in groups. Some members of your group would provide protection; others would provide or prepare food. If you were excluded from the group, you were on your own, and everything became much more complex and dangerous.

It might surprise you that there was no word for loneliness in the English language before 1800. The emergence of the word loneliness coincided with the massive social changes of the Industrial Revolution. It wasn't that loneliness didn't exist before 1800; it was that post the Industrial Revolution, it became a problem across society rather than just a problem for individuals. Loneliness has expanded as society has changed; many more people are living on their own, and there are more single-parent families and less daily face-to-face interaction.

What Keeps Us Keeps Us Healthy And Happy?

The Harvard Study of Adult Development[69] is history's most comprehensive study of human behaviour. For over seventy-five years, the project has studied a group of 724 men from their late teens and early twenties into death or old age. There are still some participants alive in their 90s. The participants were drawn from two different backgrounds: students at Harvard University, including the future President Kennedy, and young men living in deprived areas of Boston. By studying two groups with varying levels of wealth, education, and opportunity, the researchers sought to identify what was critical to people being happy and healthy over their lifetime. Participants completed questionnaires every two years about everything going on in their lives. The researchers gathered and then analysed massive amounts of data.

What Did They Find?

Good relationships keep us healthier and happier. That's the key. It wasn't wealth, success, travel, living in a beautiful house or getting to the top of your profession. It was having someone you were close to. It was being connected at a very personal level. Social connections are really good for us; sadly, loneliness kills us. People more connected to family, friends, and community tend to be happier, physically healthier, and live longer. People who are more isolated than they want to be find that they are less happy, their health declines earlier in midlife, their brain function declines earlier, and they live shorter lives.

It's not the number of your relationships – it's the quality. Living in conflict is bad for your health. Living in a marriage full of anger is worse than getting divorced. Good relationships are protective of the mind and body. Having good relationships at age 50 is the most accurate predictor of how your life will be at age 80. It isn't cholesterol levels or other physical predictors; it is simply the quality of your relationships. Those happiest in their relationships at 50 are the healthiest at age 80.

Good relationships don't just protect our bodies; they protect our brains. If you are in your 80s and in a supportive relationship, where you can count on your partner or those closest to you, your memory stays sharper longer – those who aren't suffer earlier memory decline. In the Harvard project, they found that it wasn't necessarily the most harmonious relationships that were the healthiest. Indeed, many of the healthiest couples were often bickering. But they all answered yes when asked, "Do you have someone who will look after you if you are ill or in need?"

Problems With Loneliness

➢Loneliness is associated with physical illnesses
Loneliness is associated with Alzheimer's, obesity, diabetes, high blood pressure, heart disease, and neurodegenerative diseases, and even cancer tumours can metastasise faster in lonely people.[70]

➢Loneliness can be contagious
As people become disengaged from social connections, it has a knock-on effect on their friends and families. A study into loneliness discovered that when one person became lonelier, so did their friends. It was believed that part of the reason was a domino effect. Lonely people tend to disengage and move to the edges of social networks, reducing their interactions with friends, who then feel lonelier.

➢Loneliness and stress are connected
Loneliness is associated with stress. It warns you that you are in danger because you are not in a group, which was massively safer during evolution. If you live alone, noises outside may trigger the stress response far more often than if there are other people in your home to keep you safe. Stress suppresses the immune system, so you are going to be more susceptible to physical illnesses as well as mental distress.

➢Loneliness and depression are linked

Loneliness can lead to depression, and depression can lead to loneliness. Feeling lonely is often triggered by feelings of not being a person who is worthy of being in the group. Feelings of worthlessness are a core contributor to depression. When people become depressed, they tend to break social linkages, withdraw into themselves, and increase their distance from other people.

➢Loneliness is associated with unfriendly behaviour

Being lonely often makes us feel down, self-doubting, upset, pessimistic, and overly sensitive to criticism. We may even react negatively to offers of help or expressions of concern. Unfortunately, these are not the behaviours or feelings we need to resolve our unhappiness. Often when you are lonely, people move away, believing you are an unfriendly person.

Loneliness

"Loneliness and the feeling of being unwanted is the most terrible poverty." – Mother Teresa

Feelings of loneliness is your subconscious mind telling you that you are less connected to other people than is safe. Your brain is warning you that being isolated from your 'group' is dangerous. Two things may be contributing to your feelings of loneliness:

- Social isolation: you cannot engage enough with the people you are emotionally connected to.
- Social disconnection: you are not emotionally connected to enough people.

Maybe you are feeling lonely because you have just let things slip. Feelings of isolation can motivate you to get on the phone and organise to meet a sibling, drop a friend an email, invite people over, or organise a family event or trip. Increase social contact and feelings of loneliness may reduce. But not for everyone. Maybe you feel lonely even when you are surrounded by other people. Social disconnection, being connected emotionally to too few people, can trigger thoughts that you aren't good enough or worthy of being in the group. You can be lonely because you don't think you belong; you're not good enough to belong. Loneliness can be a similar emotion to shame, the belief that you are the problem.

Below we look at reducing loneliness in two stages:

- Prepare emotionally to become connected.
- Increase your social engagement.

Stage 1: Prepare Emotionally To Become Connected

Loneliness can trigger feelings similar to shame; you believe it's your fault that you are lonely. You aren't good enough to be part of the 'group': your community, family, or team at work. You are not worthy. And it can hurt. You may have lots of social interaction through going to work, university, or school, but you still feel lonely. Many people surround you, but you have low levels of connection. You don't feel bonded to anyone, everyone is an acquaintance or colleague, not a friend, and you don't feel included. It is unlikely that further social activity will make you feel better; indeed, it could make you feel worse as you feel more and more of an outsider. It may be more effective for you to prepare emotionally before you increase your level of social engagement.

Signs that you are suffering from loneliness include:

- You may feel that none of your relationships is on a deeper, more intimate level than casual acquaintances. People are colleagues, roommates, and neighbours but nothing more. You feel disconnected in a way that is causing you to feel upset and helpless to change.

- You may have nobody you would describe as a best friend or best friends, people you feel close to.

- You feel on your own and lonely even when you are with people.

- You feel negative about yourself, feeling you aren't good enough, and that feeling lonely is your fault.

- When you try to reach out, it doesn't seem to work, and you feel even more rejected.

- You feel tired of worrying about how to become connected and what will happen to you in the future.

- You feel anxious about being rejected and often decline social invitations even though you feel lonely.

Talk To Someone About Your Loneliness

Feelings of loneliness may be combined with other issues, including depression and anxiety. Often when people are feeling distressed, it isn't easy to work out precisely what is happening. Talking to someone else can help you identify what is causing you to be distressed.

- A friend, colleague, or family member. If you have someone you trust, talk to them about how you feel. When you explain your feelings to someone else, it is different from when you hold a one-sided conversation in your mind. Often, as you describe how you are feeling, things become clearer.

- A mental health professional or advisor. If you don't have a friend or family member you feel you can talk to, or the situation needs some professional knowledge, speak to a doctor, counsellor, or advisor. You may be able to access an advisor, for example, through an Employee Assistance Programme, Community Support or Students' Advice Centre. If you are distressed, seek medical advice, and don't self-diagnose.

Whichever option you choose, talking to someone who can listen empathetically and with compassion will help to reduce your feelings of loneliness. You may find that a talking therapy, such as cognitive behaviour therapy, could prove helpful.

Identify And Challenge Your Negative Self-Talk

Practising mindfulness meditation, chapter 3, is excellent in helping you identify, understand, label, and disempower your negative thoughts and emotions. Mindfulness is the practical application of metacognition, your ability to think about your thoughts and feelings even as you have them. When you identify your negative self-talk, you can challenge and change it. Usually, our negative thoughts are not based on reality, so gathering evidence helps to reframe them into a more positive format. As with other negative self-talk, try using the triple-column technique to reframe it into more optimistic but realistic self-talk.

Identify your negative self-talk, and label it as such. Gather some objective evidence about the situation. Construct an optimistic statement: The problem is temporary, the problem is specific and contained, and the problem does not make you a bad person. This is not delusional thinking; it is simply a more optimistic framework which evidence shows is more beneficial for your mental health than a pessimistic framework.

Negative self-talk: No one likes me at work.

Evidence: Some people have been friendly to me, others more standoffish.

Positive self-talk: I am struggling to fit in at the moment at work, everything is fine at home, I am a good friend when people get to know me.

Practise Self-Compassion

Everyone hurts; it is part of being human. Hurting is not a punishment for being a bad person; it's your mind telling you that something is wrong. Everyone has flaws, makes mistakes, does silly things, and has regrets. Practising self-compassion, see chapter 7, is excellent for your physical and mental health. When you practise self-compassion, you reduce your body's level of stress.[71] Stress is the mind's response to indications of danger; the stress response is calmed when the indications are that the threat has passed. By practising self-compassion, you can reduce the times you are stressed and the degree of stress you experience and shorten the period when you are stressed. When you self-criticise, you trigger the body's stress response. Many people believe that self-criticism is a motivational tool. In very restricted circumstances, it may be. Those circumstances do not include when you are feeling isolated, lonely, hurt, and ashamed. Self-criticism will only make things much worse.

Stage 2: Increase Your Social Engagement

"You can't stay in your corner of the Forest waiting for others to come to you. You have to go to them sometimes." – Winnie the Pooh, A.A. Milne

At different times in your life, your circumstances might make it more difficult to be socially engaged. For example, university students often struggle to create social linkages in a new city, in a new way of living and studying. In middle age, social engagement may not happen as easily if there aren't young children to be taken to school, sports days, and parties. Older people may become more isolated when they retire, if their mobility is restricted, or if their partners and friends die. Many people then find it difficult to initiate new friendships, perhaps feeling awkward or vulnerable or forgetting how to do so. Here are some steps to build social engagement and increase your sense of being included.

Learn To Make New Friends

In his book, *How to Win Friends and Influence People*, Dale Carnegie gives some excellent, straightforward advice on how to make friends.[72]

➢Smile more often

It can be a habit to smile or a habit not to smile. Be a proactive smiler. If you do it often enough, you will get a positive response. Even if someone doesn't smile back the first time, it could be because they are surprised that you smiled at them. If you repeat smiling the next time you meet them, they may change their assessment of you from being the grinch to being a nice person.

The benefits of smiling are extensive:

- ✓ Smiling is correlated with living longer.[73] Happier people live longer, and happier people smile more.

- ✓ Smiling, even if it is forced, can reduce stress. Your amygdala, the centre of your stress response, can be fooled into thinking the danger has passed by smiling.

- ✓ Smiling, even if forced, can trigger the production of small amounts of dopamine and serotonin. Smiling is a natural anti-depressant.

- ✓ Smiling is contagious. Your smile can positively impact the mood of others around you. Other people smiling in response to your smile makes you feel better and more included.

- ✓ Smiling boosts the immune system. Stress weakens your immune system, so reducing your stress by smiling improves your mood and protects your physical health.

- ✓ Smiling can reduce your blood pressure. If you have a blood pressure monitor at home, try it. Take a reading, then smile for a minute and see if it changes.

- ✓ Smiling makes you more attractive.[74] People like people who smile and will keep their distance if they see scowls, frowns, or other subconscious signals to stay away.

➢Be genuinely interested in the other person

There is the old saying, "To have a friend, you must be a friend." Enduring friendships are mutually positive experiences. A key to this is empathy, developing an understanding of what it is like to be the other person. If you focus on them instead of yourself, they are more likely to be interested in a connection.

➢Remember and use someone's name

It makes a positive impact when you use someone's name. You have made an effort, which makes them feel valued. If you don't, they think you are not interested enough in them to ask or remember their name. Why should they invest in what is unlikely to be a mutually beneficial relationship?

➢**Listen and ask people questions**

Many people think that trying to make a relationship with someone involves being interesting or having something great to tell someone. It is almost the opposite: relationships are built by asking questions – and listening to people's answers.

➢**Focus on what is important to the other person**

Investing in a relationship means just that. You must be prepared to spend time understanding what is important to the other person and building a relationship that includes what is important to the other person. If you want to connect with a bird watcher, be prepared to learn about birds.

Maintain Connecting Rituals

Many happy and healthy cultures have rituals that maintain connections across a lifetime. Multiple generations of families share a meal regularly, making it natural to engage without having to initiate it constantly. Even if you are having an issue with someone, you will still meet and engage with them regularly. Playing golf every Saturday morning with the same group of friends, following your favourite football team together, or attending church activities achieves the same thing. These connecting rituals are likely to become even more important as higher numbers of people live on their own and more people work from home. Many people understand this and choose to undertake activities in groups that could easily be done independently. Running, cycling, and sea swimming groups are thriving; people know the value of this social engagement to their physical and mental health.

Talk To People

Researchers found that even engaging with acquaintances, what they called weak ties, contributes to our mental health.[75] There are many opportunities in our daily lives to engage with other human beings, even people we don't know. How often do you chat with the person at the checkout desk in the supermarket? Talk to them; it will benefit you and maybe brighten your day. Do you talk to anyone when you are queueing for your coffee or do you make it clear you want zero social interaction? What about if you get a taxi? Do you interact with the driver or use Uber's Quiet Mode, which warns the driver you're not interested in talking? Or do you think that engaging through social media replaces human interaction? A study at the University of Pennsylvania found that reducing social media to thirty minutes a day significantly reduced loneliness and depression.[76] Human beings are hotwired to connect, especially face to face. Even casual conversations can make you feel included, and maintain skills you might need if your circumstances become more challenging.

I was walking on the beach, and as happens occasionally, there was a man with a metal detector and a spade. If I had given him any thought on previous occasions, to be honest, I would not have expected that it would be an opportunity for a great conversation. But I decided to shout down to him from the sea wall and I asked him if he had found much. He said actually today was a very good day. I thought he was going to tell me how many pound coins he had found lost by beach users the previous day. Instead, he showed me an Edward VII silver sixpence and a gold wedding ring. The sixpence was only worth the small amount of silver it contained, but the ring was more important. It was gold with a small diamond. The diamond was attached to the gold by a small blob of black material – I think he said it was bitumen. This dated the ring to the 1800s. I went off, delighted to have had the chat and intrigued to think how this wedding band ended up on Ballyholme beach two hundred years later. This unexpected encounter went into my gratitude diary and increased my positivity ratio for the rest of the day. I was also able to enter in my gratitude diary that this positive event happened because I initiated it: I had said hello.

There is an interesting TEDx video by Dr Olivia Remes, a mental health researcher at the University of Cambridge called "How to get rid of loneliness and become happy", see link in resources at the end of the chapter. She advises to do two things:

1. Talk to everyone, everywhere, and
2. Be more open about yourself.

Get A Dog (Maybe A Cat)

Having a pet can give us some of the connections we need. Petting an animal triggers the production of oxytocin, the bonding hormone, at similar levels to engaging with another human. Dogs give us unconditional love, which we may struggle to receive through human relationships in our lives. Dogs also need to be fed and walked, which increases daily engagement opportunities. Many people are more comfortable talking with another dog owner than someone on their own. It is easy and acceptable to compliment a stranger's dog. The response would be completely different if you complimented a stranger's own appearance.

Summary

- The key to living a happy and healthy life is being connected to other people, our friends, family, and community.

- Humans are hardwired to be connected in groups, contributing to the species' survival.

- If we do not have enough social interaction, we can feel isolated and stressed.

- The absence of social connection triggers feelings of loneliness; loneliness is connected to shame.

- Preparing emotionally can allow us to re-engage positively.

- You can take simple steps to increase your social engagement and connection.

Resources

- Psychiatrist Robert Waldinger explains the findings of the Harvard Study of Adult Development in an engaging 12-minute video. https://www.youtube.com/watch?v=8KkKuTCFvzI

- Excellent video about how people live to be 100 by psychologist and journalist Susan Pinker, author of The Village Effect. She researched why so many people live to a great age in Villagrande in Sardinia's blue zone (geographic locations of longevity clusters) https://www.youtube.com/watch?v=ptIecdCZ3dg

- 5-minute video explanation of what having a dog does to your brain https://www.youtube.com/watch?v=w0K6UBzGQ7E

- TEDx talk by Dr Olivia Remes, "How to get rid of loneliness and become happy": https://www.youtube.com/watch?v=vZT-bB66iIk

Next Chapter

Being mentally healthy means that you do not become ill every time something goes wrong in your life. Mentally healthy people are resilient; they bounce back after an adverse event and continue forward even when there are barriers.

CHAPTER 9: BEING RESILIENT

"I can be changed by what happens to me. But I refuse to be reduced by it." – Maya Angelou

Mental health isn't fragile; it's resilient. Being resilient means you deal with stress, not just avoid it. You make mistakes, and you learn from them. You make bad decisions, but you don't give up. Life bruises you, but it doesn't defeat you. Things go wrong in life; you fail an exam, you fail in a relationship, you fail in a job, but you don't become a failure. That's resilience; it's your refusal to be reduced by life.As Samuel Beckett said, "Ever tried, ever failed, no matter, try again, fail again, fail better".

Problems Associated With Low Resilience

➢ Difficulty in managing stress can lead to high blood pressure, weakened immune system, anxiety, depression, insomnia, and heart disease.[77]

➢ Increased likelihood of giving up before resolving a problem or achieving a goal.

➢ Tendency to ruminate about negative events in your life leading to ongoing distress.

➢ Grudge-holding, being unable to forgive and move on.

➢ Unhealthy coping mechanisms including substance abuse, eating disorders, and risk-taking behaviours.

Emotional Resilience

Your emotional resilience is how you react and adapt to adverse events happening in your life. If you are emotionally resilient, you do three things in response to negative events. You keep going, you recover emotionally, and you grow.[78]

1. Keep going

> *"Our greatest weakness lies in giving up. The most certain way to succeed is always to try just one more time." – Thomas Edison*

You continue; you don't give up. Psychologists refer to this as sustainability, the ability to continue forward during difficult times. If you give up when you get upset, you can begin to feel helpless because you aren't able to achieve your goals or solve your problems. Feelings of helplessness are closely associated with depression; some psychologists think of depression as learned helplessness. When a reporter asked Thomas Edison, the inventor of the first working lightbulb, "How did it feel to fail 1,000 times?" Edison replied, "I didn't fail 1,000 times. The light bulb was an invention with 1,000 steps.[79] Great success is built on failure, frustration, even catastrophe."

2. Recover emotionally

> *"Do not judge me by my success; judge me by how many times I fell down and got back up again." – Nelson Mandela*

Resilience is not about trying to avoid getting upset. Resilient people get upset when a negative event happens like anyone else, but then they recover. Everyone gets upset when they experience a negative event. You could feel disappointed, stressed, angry, traumatised, let down, embarrassed, or frightened. You don't become resilient by trying to avoid or deny these natural emotions; you become resilient by controlling your reaction to these negative emotions. If you get a parking ticket and are resilient, you could be upset for an hour and then move on. If you are resilient and lose your job, you could be upset for a week, but then you recover emotionally and start to plan what to do next.

What highly resilient people avoid doing is ruminating, going over and over the adverse event in their mind time after time. Remembering a negative event can trigger the same stressful, emotional response as if it was happening to you right now. If you ruminate over one negative event multiple times, you trigger numerous negative emotional reactions to a single negative event. This is devastating to your positivity ratio discussed in chapter 1. People with lower levels of emotional resilience tend to be ruminators. Imagine you arrive at work, and someone has sent you an abusive email. Instead of processing your upset, you ruminate about the event that triggered the upset. Whenever you think of the email, you get as upset as when you first read it. And if you're upset when you reply to the email, you may say something that makes the whole situation more upsetting. A highly resilient person will be upset about the email and then move on; they will have recovered emotionally and are no longer stressed about it.

3. Grow

If you face difficulties and succeed in overcoming them, you aren't the same person. You learn from the mistakes you make in life. The German philosopher Nietzsche said, "That which does not kill us makes us stronger". If you have healthy emotional resilience, you learn from your struggles. You don't give up, you control your emotional response, and succeed despite your difficulties. Success breeds success. Another time, Edison said, "I have not failed, not once, I've discovered ten thousand ways that don't work".[80] That's resilience. Unfortunately, if you have low levels of emotional resilience, you learn the opposite. You are helpless because you give up too quickly, you may feel hopeless because you ruminate and catastrophise about the negative events in your life, and you may become worn down by life's challenges. Low resilience is associated with a higher risk of depression.

Becoming More Resilient

Somewhere between 25 per cent and 40 per cent of your emotional resilience is estimated to be genetic. This portion of your resilience is fixed, leaving well over half of your emotional resilience that can be changed. You may think of yourself as someone with low resilience, but it would be more accurate to think of yourself as someone with currently low resilience. The evidence is clear: you can build emotional resilience by developing your ability to cope healthily when negative things happen. You may think of yourself as a highly resilient person, but it would be more accurate to think of yourself as currently highly resilient. Even people with high resilience can be affected by overwork, illness, ongoing stress, or trauma. Everyone should invest in their emotional resilience to protect it and their mental health. Emotional resilience is how you react to negative events. The following is a four-step sequence that can help you to respond consistently in a resilient manner to negative events.

COPE – [Control Optimism Plan Execute]

Step 1: Control your response to your emotions, not your emotions

When something goes wrong in your life, the first thing that happens is that you have an emotional response to the negative or threatening event. This is your fight or flight response, your stress response, which could save your life in a situation of real danger. When you are stressed, you react emotionally. You take immediate action to escape or attack the source of danger. It's not thinking about what you should do; it's about quick and dramatic action. In genuine times of danger, this dramatic, emotional reaction is much more likely to keep you safe than trying to develop a thought-through plan.

Your stress response is controlled by a part of your brain called the amygdala. The amygdala's primary job is to get you to move away from or attack the source of danger as fast as possible. It triggers the production of cortisol, the stress hormone, and adrenaline so that you have the drive and the energy to respond to imminent danger quickly. There is, however, a significant problem. The amygdala is not really able to distinguish between a life and death situation and an upsetting one. It can trigger your stress response when you are not in physical danger; when you suffer a failure, you make a mistake, you're asked to present to the team, or someone is rude to you or sends a nasty email. It's why you want to get up and physically move away from a problem or lash out at someone.

Stress also causes us to catastrophise. If you suspect that there is a bear behind the bush, it makes sense for your survival to go with the most dangerous alternative. So, you tend to catastrophise when stressed – if it turns out not to have been a bear, well, better safe than sorry, you're still alive. Unfortunately, in modern times, the stress response is a significant killer, bears not so much. Mindfulness, see chapter 3, empowers you to manage your response to being stressed. It's not managing your stress response; the amygdala controls that. Being resilient isn't about avoiding getting upset or stressed; it's about controlling what you do while you are upset and stressed.

Mindfulness meditation trains you to observe your thoughts and emotions without being owned by them. By focusing on your breathing, you can become an observer of your thoughts and feelings. Without practising mindfulness, you may be automatically responding to higher levels of cortisol and adrenaline – losing your temper, wanting to lash out, catastrophising, jumping to wrong conclusions, feeling a failure, blaming everyone but yourself, feeling guilty or even ashamed. It's difficult to minimise, control, or avoid these emotions when triggered by your amygdala: they are hardwired into your brain. By practising mindfulness, however, you learn to identify these emotions and control your reaction to them. This may not be easy, but you will get better with regular practice.

➢ **Use Viktor Frankl's space to choose your response**

Viktor Frankl was a world-famous Austrian psychiatrist who founded the logotherapy school of psychotherapy. During the Second World War, he survived being interned in four concentration camps, including Auschwitz. How Frankl survived where many didn't is described in his seminal book, *Man's Search for Meaning*.[81] One of his most famous quotes about how he survived is relevant in helping us to become more resilient: "Between stimulus and response, there is a space. In that space is our power to choose our response. In our response lies our growth and our freedom."

If you react without thinking when you become stressed, you are responding to the stress stimulus with an emotional reaction. You make bad decisions and often lose control of what happens next. You become upset, storm off, send an email that is way out of line, or say something unacceptable. Immediately you regret what you have done, but unfortunately, you have now lost control of the situation and what happens next. If you have practised mindfulness, you are not controlled by the emotions triggered by the release of cortisol. If you can separate your rational thoughts from your emotions, you can choose what you want the outcome of this situation to be. If you don't practise mindfulness, take time out. Go for a brisk walk, your cortisol and adrenaline levels will begin to reduce, and then you will start to think rationally again. You are also less likely to give up because you are no longer overwhelmed. Focus on identifying your stress response and the emotions it is generating. Recognise what it is but then stop. Stop and think rationally about what you want to happen next, your rational thought-through response – that's you on the first step to becoming more resilient.

Step 2: Optimism, Optimistic Reframing

When something goes wrong in your life, you explain what has happened in either an optimistic or a pessimistic style. There is overwhelming evidence that using an optimistic explanatory style leads to more positive outcomes across your lifetime. An optimist looks at a problem and thinks three things:

➢**The problem is temporary and will end**

Imagine you have just received the results of a university examination. Unfortunately, you have failed. A pessimist will often explain their failures in a permanent way – "I failed the exam because I'm not clever enough". You can't do much about that, so you might as well give up! An optimist is likelier to say, "I should have studied harder, I will make more of an effort next term, and I will pass the re-sit". Look at the problem you are facing and see it as something that will pass. You may not know how or when it will pass, but it will pass.

➢**It's specific, it's what it is and no more**

Pessimists often make emotional mountains out of molehills: they catastrophise. "I failed one exam, so I'm going to fail all the exams". Did you ever hear the saying bad things come in threes? Well, they don't – the tendency to see unrelated connections is called 'apophenia', contributing to catastrophising and depression. Optimists see problems as being specific, not global. "I failed the chemistry exam because I hate chemistry; I'll pass the rest of them"; "I'm not good at presentations, but I'm great at talking one-to-one". Look at the problem you are facing and see it as it is, not exaggerated by your stress.

➢A mistake doesn't make you a failure

Pessimists tend to blame themselves automatically. You may have made a mistake, but that doesn't make you a bad person or a failure. You may feel guilty about your role in this negative event, but that shows your empathy; you understand that you have made a bad decision or an error. Remember Teddy Roosevelt's "Man in the Arena" speech (chapter 6), and don't be the cheerleader for your critics. Accept that you may have contributed to the negative event; you will help to repair the consequences of what you are responsible for and learn from it. Practice self-compassion as discussed in chapter 7; it is going to be much more beneficial to your mental health than self-criticism. Self-criticism only makes you feel worse and doesn't motivate you to improve.

Step 3: Plan

If you want to achieve something, you need to know what it is. This is a particular issue when you are stressed. Your amygdala tells you to run in any direction and climb a tree, hide under a bush, get a spear, or lie down and pretend to be dead. Do anything but just get away from the danger. The stress response is powerful but focused on reacting to danger and is primitive and outdated. The vast majority of times, when stressed, we are not in physical danger, so the stress response is often a burden, not a benefit. You are much more likely to bounce back emotionally and sustain your actions if you know what you are trying to achieve.

When stressed and emotional, the most straightforward plan is to focus on your desired vision

Sometimes you cannot develop a detailed action plan because the situation is too stressful, too complicated, too fluid, too opaque, or too emotional. In that case, your plan will have only one element: the vision of the future you want. Keep focusing on your vision until it becomes clearer how to achieve it.

- ➢You are asked to do a presentation to the whole team. **Vision**: you will have delivered a competent presentation of which you're proud.

- ➢You have received an aggressive email from a colleague. **Vision**: you will have resolved the situation without it escalating into a personal dispute.

- ➢You missed your flight. **Vision**: you will have got home safely without colossal expense, exhaustion, or distress.

By focusing on your vision rather than your feelings, you initiate a thought-through response rather than an emotional reaction. Often you can see this behaviour in people you would think of as leaders. They stay focused on what needs to be achieved. As Rudyard Kipling said in the first line of his poem, "If you can keep your head when all about you are losing theirs". Keep your head by focusing on your vision until your stress response calms down.

Build a more detailed plan backwards from your vision

Start in the future and then walk backwards to today. What is your vision, what must change if you are to achieve your vision, what actions can bring about these changes, and what resources do you need to deliver these actions successfully? Simple straightforward questions will help you to come up with an effective plan.

Step 4: Execute

You are asked to do a presentation at work. You feel overwhelmed by your stress response, and in your mind's eye, you can see the humiliation coming your way, not being able to face your colleagues and maybe having to give up your job after a horrendous exhibition of incoherence and incompetence.

Control your response to your stress

Having practised mindfulness, you can recognise that your stress response has triggered these thoughts and emotions. Simply observe and label your emotions, don't let them cause you to react emotionally. Go for a brisk walk and reduce the level of cortisol and adrenaline in your bloodstream.

Optimistic Reframing

This is a temporary problem that you will move through, it is a specific task that you have been asked to complete, which is not threatening your whole career, and you are far from the only person at work who is nervous around public speaking.

Plan

Draw up your plan, starting with your vision and working backwards.

Vision: I will have delivered a competent presentation of which I am proud.

Change1: I will have a comprehensive professional PowerPoint Presentation developed in plenty of time.

Actions: I will structure my content. I will develop the slides to present the content coherently.

Change 2: I will have practised my delivery so that I am sure I can do it competently.

Actions: I will practise in the board room where it will be delivered, so I am accustomed to and comfortable with the set-up. I will practise in front of a small group of friends and get feedback.

Resources: Jenny is great at doing presentations: she will help me. I need to book the boardroom to practise. Need laptop, projector, and wireless presentation changer.

Execute

Talk to Jenny and ask for her help and guidance. Develop the PowerPoint with Jenny's help. Book the board room, get the equipment and become comfortable using it. Practise delivering to a small group and get feedback. Keep your vision front and centre. Practise mindfulness, separating your stress emotions from yourself. Deliver, and do a good job. Grow as a person. Celebrate!

Avoid Unhealthy Coping Strategies

Just because a behaviour helps you to endure emotional pain doesn't mean it's healthy. Some coping behaviours are unhealthy and are likely to lead to lower levels of resilience. Here are some unhealthy coping skills:

Drinking alcohol or using drugs: Substances may temporarily numb your pain, but they won't resolve your issues. Substances are likely to introduce new problems into your life. Alcohol, for example, is a depressant that can make you feel worse. Using substances to cope also puts you at risk of developing a substance use disorder and may create health, legal, financial, and social problems.

Overeating: Food is a common coping strategy. But, trying to 'stuff your feelings' with food can lead to an unhealthy relationship with food and health issues. Sometimes people go to the other extreme and restrict their eating because it makes them feel more in control, which can be just as unhealthy.

Sleeping too much: Whether you nap when stressed out or sleep late to avoid facing the day, sleeping offers a temporary escape from your problems. However, when you wake up, the problem will still be there.

Constantly complaining to others: Talking about your problems to gain support, develop a solution, or see a problem differently can be healthy. But studies show that repeatedly venting to people about how bad your situation is or how terrible you feel is more likely to keep you stuck in a place of pain.

Recklessly overspending: While many say they enjoy retail therapy to feel better, shopping can become unhealthy. Owning too many possessions can add stress to your life. Also, spending more than you can afford will only backfire and cause more stress.

Avoiding the problem: Even 'healthy' coping strategies can become unhealthy if you use them to avoid the problem. For example, if you are stressed about your financial situation, you might be tempted to spend time with friends or watch TV because that's less anxiety-provoking than creating a budget. But if you never resolve your financial issues, your coping strategies will only mask the problem.

Summary

- ➢Recovery is the ability to bounce back emotionally after a negative event.

- ➢Sustainability is the ability to continue through difficulties to achieve your goals or solve your problems.

- ➢Facing and overcoming difficulties in life changes you and helps you to grow.

- ➢You can learn to respond in a consistently more resilient way to negative events using COPE
    - **C**ontrol your response to your emotions, not your emotions.
    - **O**ptimistic reframing, the problem is temporary, specific, and doesn't mean I'm a failure.
    - **P**lan, start with a clear vision of what it will be like when you succeed and then work your steps backwards to today.
    - **E**xecute, actions bring about change, not words, plans or emotions.

- ➢Avoid unhealthy coping strategies, including alcohol, food, oversleeping, overspending, and avoidance.

Resources

- ➢Self-score your emotional resilience using the Brief Resilience Scale. https://ogg.osu.edu/media/documents/MB%20Stream/Brief%20Resilience%20Scale.pdf

- ➢The American Psychological Society has a range of interesting and relevant articles at https://www.apa.org/topics/resilience

- ➢TEDx talk by Raphael Rose of UCLA 'From stress to resilience'. He talks about what stresses astronauts and what we can learn from them. https://www.youtube.com/watch?v=Q7vYuKvpneM.

- ➢TEDx talk by neuroscientist Kristen Race "Generation stress: From surviving to thriving". Small changes bring sustained change. https://www.youtube.com/watch?v=7jRND5IU3Qg

Next Chapter

Your journey to mental health is unique. But there are core habits you should incorporate into your day, such as gratitude, mindfulness, and kindness, which will benefit you. You may also have a more specific barrier to mental health, which you should be able to identify by asking a series of linked questions.

CHAPTER 10: BECOMING MENTALLY HEALTHY

"I wonder why things have to change," murmured Piglet. Pooh thought for a while, then said, "It gives them a chance to get better." – A.A. Milne

If you want to become mentally healthy, some basic practices, such as keeping a gratitude diary, will benefit you. You don't need to overthink: start doing them, and you will benefit from them. Other practices will only be of value if you have a particular issue: for example, if you have healthy self-confidence, investing in trying to develop further self-confidence may not be that useful, but if you are affected by imposter syndrome, you may benefit substantially by identifying and addressing this specific barrier to having flourishing mental health.

Therefore, you may benefit from following a two-phase approach to becoming mentally healthy:

- **Phase 1** is to incorporate seven core habits of mentally healthy people into your daily life and start today! Just start doing them and make them a part of your daily routine. They are the emotional equivalent of eating healthily, brushing your teeth, and exercising. Everyone should do them. You don't need a plan. Just start doing them now. They also contain skills that you may need in phase 2.

- **Phase 2** is more individual, and not everyone needs to have a phase 2. The seven habits you introduce in phase 1, such as mindfulness meditation, empower your subconscious mind to resolve and prevent many mental health issues. However, if you find that you are still experiencing a barrier to becoming mentally healthy, you may need to develop and implement phase 2.

Phase 1: Practise The Seven Habits Of Mentally Healthy People: Start Today

"You don't have to see the whole staircase, just take the first step." – Martin Luther King Jr

You are stressed, always busy, and too many people need a part of you. You haven't got time for your coffee break, never mind sitting down and developing an integrated mental health strategy. You want to start doing something today that starts to improve your mental health immediately. It can't take up much time because you just don't have any spare time. But you would like to start your journey towards better mental health on a sound, scientific basis. Thankfully you can incorporate small, repeatable actions in your daily life and start benefiting from them quickly.

Habit 1: Keep a gratitude diary, chapter 2

Keeping a gratitude diary is a fabulous place to start if you aren't already doing so. It only takes five minutes a day. Do it this evening before going to sleep. Use an online gratitude app or simply list three things to be grateful for, using paper and a pen, and then throw the list away as it has nothing to do with record-keeping.

Keeping a gratitude diary is going to achieve two things for you:

- You will experience a higher positivity ratio without changing anything else in your life. You will feel happier even though your life hasn't changed; it is your brain that has changed.
- You are going to have demonstrated that neuroplasticity works for you. The physical activity of writing or typing three things you are grateful for changes your brain's focus and activity. Your subconscious brain scans more actively for positive events and celebrates them more strongly when it finds them.

If you already use a gratitude diary, you could consider expressing your gratitude to someone each day whom you would not normally thank. You could also expand your gratitude diary by recording one further thing: why the good thing happened. You may be surprised how often an act of yours leads to a positive event.

Habit 2: Mindfulness meditation, chapter 3

Mindfulness is an emotional superpower. You can change your mental health by meditating for ten minutes a day. Mindfulness is far more than a relaxing exercise; it causes changes in how your brain functions. Researchers can see the changes in people's brains using fMRI scanners. You can learn to stop running on automatic pilot and being controlled by your stress. Mindfulness meditation is part of our self-soothing process; by practising it, you are deactivating the stress response. There are many free mindfulness meditation resources online.

Habit 3: Mindful physical activity, chapter 3

A 30-minute investment every day in physical activity will contribute to the achievement and protection of your mental health. You may find that one form of exercise is more mindful for you than others. Walking the dog, walking in a park or on the beach, swimming, running, or cycling are all potential mindful activities. What form of activity effectively counteracts your stress, anxiety, or depressive thoughts?

For me, it is swimming. I benefit from swimming much more than any other form of physical activity. And the emotional benefits last for far longer. If I can't get for a swim, walking the dogs is a great substitute. What works best for you? Plan it in your day and be proactive. If you don't build it into your plan other things will take preference, like non-urgent emails, or looking at LinkedIn.

Habit 4: Perform an act of kindness daily, chapter 3

If you want to be happier this afternoon, do an act of kindness this afternoon. If you build one act of genuine kindness into every day of your life, you will be happier and less lonely. Your brain will release dopamine and oxytocin.

- Send a text to someone and thank them for helping you.
- Make your colleague a cup of coffee.
- Bake a cake and bring it to work.
- Listen to someone with empathy instead of giving advice.
- Volunteer at an animal shelter, charity shop, drop-in centre, or support service.
- Donate to a charity.

Habit 5: Plan a hedonic moment into your day, every day, chapter 3

Think of tomorrow and plan some events that are going to make you feel better:

- Walk the dogs
- Eat your favourite meal
- Read for an hour
- Weed the garden
- Crochet a hat

What makes you feel good? Do it and feel good! Plan it the same as all the tasks you have to complete that aren't going to make you feel better. Build 'hedonic' well-being in your daily life. It's not selfish; it's mentally healthy!

Habit 6: Practise optimism, chapter 4

You may not think of yourself as a pessimist; maybe you consider yourself more of a realist. Unfortunately, that doesn't mean you aren't using a pessimistic explanatory style. It's a behaviour you may have learned as a young child and are using automatically subconsciously.

If you use mindfulness meditation, you will become competent in identifying your pessimistic thought pattern. Change your thought pattern to an optimistic framing:

- A problem is temporary: at some stage, it will cease to be a problem. I will pass the exam next time.
- A problem is specific, it does not need to be a catastrophe, and bad things do not come in threes. I failed chemistry but passed the rest.
- A mistake does not make you a bad person. Learn from it, 'fail better'. I can focus on chemistry as my weakest subject.

Habit 7: Practise self-compassion, chapter 7

Many people have internal self-talk that they would not accept from anyone else. Self-criticism does not motivate you; it makes you emotionally unwell.

Mindfulness will help you to identify and label negative self-talk, but you can go further. Complete Dr Kristin Neff's Self-Compassion online test: https://self-compassion.org/self-compassion-test/ Immediately below the results on her website is a link to a list of resources you can download – most are audio or video resources to help you to be kinder to yourself.

- Be kind to yourself; talk to yourself as a friend.
- Others share your problems; other people can help.
- Identify, don't ignore but also don't be owned by, your thoughts and emotions.

Phase 2: Addressing Personal Barriers To Mental Health

Your life is different from everyone else's, and so is your mental health. The core habits you have implemented in phase 1 will help you on your journey to mental health, but you may have additional barriers that require more attention. Do allow the habits from phase 1 to start benefiting you before completing this phase, as there is a delay between implementing a new habit and it beginning to help you. For example, using a gratitude diary does not change your subconscious for at least a week and a half, and you need to let it do its work. The same with mindfulness meditation: it is core to challenging negative self-talk, but it takes time. If you tried to address all of the issues discussed in this book together, it would be overwhelming. It is likely to be more effective if you identify one or two issues that are causing you distress and acting as a barrier to you becoming mentally healthy. A strategic approach is to ask the following linked questions, which will help you to identify a plan to move forward.

Question One: Is An Illness Stopping You From Becoming Mentally Healthy?

You cannot be mentally healthy if you are suffering from a common mental health disorder. Therefore, you first need to consider whether you are suffering from an illness such as clinical depression or an anxiety disorder. If you are concerned, talk to an appropriate health professional and get a proper assessment: don't self-diagnose. Ignoring an illness like depression is likely to increase the severity of the symptoms, lengthen the recovery time, and increase the chance you will develop a second illness.

The good news is that about 80 per cent of people will start to respond to treatment for illnesses such as clinical depression in four to six weeks. That does not mean you have fully recovered, but that you are on the journey to recovery. As you recover, you can start to move towards mental health by using the evidence-supported activities discussed in this book, including the seven habits listed above. If you don't invest in these habits, you may become stuck in lethargic mental health – you have recovered from being depressed, but you are not mentally healthy. A significant benefit of achieving flourishing mental health is that you are up to six times less likely to return to being clinically depressed than if you have languishing mental health.[82]

Question Two: To Become Mentally Healthy, What Must Change?

If necessary, you have checked with a health professional, and you're not suffering from an illness. Still, you are suffering a level of emotional distress that is preventing you from attaining flourishing mental health. The next step is to identify the source of your distress and what is the barrier that is preventing you from achieving flourishing mental health.

Ask

- Do I need to feel happier more often?
- Do I need to have a healthier level of self-worth?
- Do I need to be more connected with people in my life?
- Do I need to be more resilient?

It is essential to focus on what needs to change, rather than what it would be nice to change. You are trying to identify a source of stress, a barrier to achieving mental health, so that you can develop a plan of action to reduce or eliminate it. If you acknowledge that you have a source of distress affecting your mental health but can't identify it, seek help. Consult a counsellor or other health professional. They can help you to explore issues in your life that you find difficult or distressful. You don't have to be ill to benefit from talking therapy or engaging with a professional listener.

Question Three: What Actions Can You Take To Remove Or Reduce The Identified Barrier?

Hopefully, you have been able to identify the area

of your mental health that is the source of your distress. Revisit the chapters that explore this area of your mental health and identify actions that evidence suggests can help improve matters.

Change needed: I need to feel happier more often.

Read chapters: 2, 3 & 4

Potential actions: Gratitude diary; Forgiveness; Self-forgiveness; Mindfulness; Kindness; Plan hedonic moments; Optimism.

Change needed: I need to have a healthier level of self-worth.

Read chapters: 5 & 6

Potential actions: Stop self-criticism; Identify perfectionist behaviour and act; Identify imposter syndrome behaviours and act; Introduce more purpose in your life.

Change needed: I need to be more connected with people in my life.

Read chapters: 7 & 8

Potential actions: Develop empathy; Compassion; Self-compassion; Smile more;

Remember and use people's names; Take a genuine interest in other people: Listen more, ask more questions.

Change needed: I need to be more resilient.

Read chapter: 9

Potential actions: Reduce rumination; Control your reaction to emotions, not your emotions; Optimistic reframing; Plan; Execute; Proactively ask for help; Focus on not giving up; Focus on your vision of the future.

Question Four: What Skills Do You Need To Achieve Mental Health?

The skills you need will vary from person to person and from strategy to strategy. However, some core skills are worth considering for your journey to mental health.

- **Being Mindful.** Mindfulness meditation will train you to be mindful. Being mindful is the practical application of metacognition, our ability to think about our thoughts even as we are thinking them, and meta-emotion, our ability to recognise our emotions even as we are experiencing them. Mindfulness is critical to separating us, as physical human beings, from our thoughts and feelings – the power of your negative thoughts and emotions is materially diminished by mindfulness. Being mindful reduces the impact of stressful, depressive, and anxious thoughts.

➢ **Empathetic, active listening.** Linking your questions to another person's answers makes you a competent listener. Asking open questions, questions which can't be answered with yes or no, also builds our competence as listeners. If you develop and use your active listening skills, you will understand other people more, develop empathy and compassion, reduce conflict, and build connections.

➢ **Emotional Control.** Learning to use Viktor Frankl's space, the space between stimulus and response, is empowering. Your emotional reaction is often not the best response. You are reacting as if you are facing a bear instead of an irritation. Process the stress and then think through what you want the outcome of the situation to be. Learn to have a thought-through response instead of an emotional reaction.

Question Five: What Help Can I Access?

One of the significant core differences between high and low resilience is being proactive in accessing help. Highly resilient people are usually the first in the queue for help; sadly, people with low resilience, who may need it more, often aren't in the queue at all. Many people with low resilience think accessing help is a sign of weakness; people with high resilience understand it's empowering.

People Can Help

➢ Someone you trust, who is an empathetic, active listener; someone who will help you to process your thoughts without judgement or prescribed solutions. They may be a family member, a friend, or a work colleague.

➢ Someone who has experienced similar issues to yours, maybe someone who has experienced imposter syndrome, or compassion fatigue, could be a great listener but also be able to share their experience of recovery.

➢ A counsellor can act as a coach. You don't need to be ill to benefit from using a counsellor. They are professional listeners who can help you talk. They can teach you techniques which will help you to achieve mental health.

Organisations Can Help

➢ Schools often provide high levels of pastoral care. If a child is struggling and affecting your mental health, engage with the school.

➢Employers may provide an Employee Assistance Programme which gives free access to counselling and other support.

➢Profession-specific charitable support. In the UK, for example, Police Officers and Staff can access help through Police Care UK; Veterinary staff can access help through VetLife.

➢Specialised charities such as in the UK MIND (mental health), CRUSE (Bereavement) and Nexus (sexual trauma).

Resources

➢YouTube has a great library of videos on mental health, including many of the world's leading researchers developing our understanding of mental health.

➢TEDx talks

➢Gratitude apps – allow you to enter the three positive events for which you are grateful.

➢Steps apps – measure the number of steps you take every day

➢Sources of online mindfulness meditations such as www.franticworld.com There are lots of free and paid resources that can help you to make your strategy a success.

- Scales such as the Warwick-Edinburgh Mental Wellbeing Scale and the Clance IP Scale.

Motivating Yourself To Improve And Protect Your Mental Health

"An ounce of action is worth a ton of theory." – Ralph Waldo Emerson

A plan only works when you put it into practice. Start practising the seven habits, and the evidence is that your mental health will improve. Many of the seven habits are enjoyable or relaxing; I often fall asleep while listening to a mindfulness meditation session. At the same time, you are learning skills such as reframing negative self-talk that you need to address conditions such as imposter syndrome. Ask for help. Maybe things won't work the first time, but learn from what you try. And then fail better until you succeed. Dr Tali Sharot, a neuroscientist at University College London, has a second excellent TEDx talk, (see chapter 4 resources for the other one). This second talk is called "How to motivate yourself to change your behaviour": https://www.youtube.com/watch?v=xp0O2vi8DX4.

Dr Sharot explains three things that neuroscience tells us will motivate us to make positive changes in our behaviours:

- Social incentives. Other people's opinions do

matter, so getting positive reactions, support, and encouragement from family, friends and colleagues are really important. Being able to show others that you are succeeding is a great motivator. Self-criticism, or being engaged with people who criticise you, is demotivational.

- Immediate rewards. A bird in the hand is worth two in the bush. An act of kindness makes you feel good now, keeping a gratitude diary brings quick benefits, and mindfulness meditation relaxes you now.
- Progress monitoring. I use a step app to measure the number of steps I take a day, and I set it at 5,000 because I want to succeed. Use the Warwick-Edinburgh Mental Wellbeing Scale to monitor your progress towards mental health. Use www.positivityratio.com to measure your positivity ratio. Success does breed success.

Dr Sharot sums it up as this: the fear of losing induces inaction, and the expectation of benefiting triggers action. Focus on the benefits that having flourishing mental health will bring. That will motivate you far more than trying to avoid mental illness. Start including the habits of mentally healthy people in your daily life with the fully realistic expectation of becoming mentally healthier.

Your Body And Mind Work Together

I wanted to finish the book with something that you would find useful immediately, and perhaps you wouldn't be aware of. Something that you could take away from reading the book that would make a difference, today. I searched my memory for something that really changed how I understood mental health and settled on a TEDx talk, in two parts, by Dr Alan Watkins, a physician and neuroscientist (see links below).

At the time I first watched the TEDx talks, I was delivering my suicide prevention programme "Mind Your Mate" every Friday morning in Hydebank Young Offenders Centre, a prison on the outskirts of Belfast. To say the young men were not a receptive audience is an understatement. Usually, all they did was put their heads down on the desk for the whole session, never made eye contact and I spent two hours talking to the tops of their heads.

In his TEDx talks, Dr Watkins uses a simple heart monitor that attaches to your ear, you plug it into your laptop, and you can show someone's heartbeat live through a projector onto a screen. I purchased one of the monitors and brought it with me the next Friday. I asked for a volunteer, attached the monitor to his ear and there was his heartbeat on the screen.

I then, copying Dr Watkins, got the young man to count backwards in threes and at the same time started stressing him by shouting random numbers at him. His heartbeat soared and became very erratic. I then asked him to start to breathe very rhythmically - breathe in for a count of five, breathe out for a count of five. As the volunteer started to breathe rhythmically his heart started to do the same thing – it reduced the average number of heartbeats per minute, but the shape of the wave pattern also changed. It became far smoother. The volunteer became less stressed because by controlling his breathing he could directly reduce the impact of his stress response.

In my mind, I have a little heart monitor and when cortisol enters my bloodstream, I see the erratic and faster heartbeat that it causes. And then as advised by Viktor Frankl I think of my response. My response to stress is to control my breathing, to breathe regularly and to identify what my thoughts are – which often include catastrophisation. And then I choose not to catastrophise.

In the second part of his TEDx talk, Dr Watkins explains how different chemicals including cortisol, adrenalin, DHEA, and ACH determine our emotional and physical state. If you become stressed, it has a very negative impact on your performance, your memory is impaired, and you make really bad decisions. If you don't perform well in exams because of stress, if you would rather die than deliver a speech to a group, or if you never perform well under pressure, this talk is going to help you. He explains that by changing your breathing you can start moving towards being in control even if you are currently agitated or stressed. Rhythmic breathing will change your heartbeat which will trigger your soothing response.

The links to the TEDx talks are:

Part 1: https://www.youtube.com/watch?v=q06YIWCR2Js

Part 2: https://www.youtube.com/watch?v=Q_fFattg8N0

Good Luck!

There are two things I love about delivering mental health training. The first is that the vast majority of people interested in learning about mental health are lovely human beings who are great to meet. The second is that people change very quickly when they are given the information they need. I genuinely hope this book will help you to improve and protect your mental health. Thanks for reading it.

[1] Gerben J. Westerhof and Corey L. M. Keyes, "Mental illness and mental health", 2010.
[2] https://www.bbc.co.uk/news/world-us-canada-27610770.
[3] Corey L. M. Keyes, "The mental health continuum: from languishing to flourishing in life", 2002.
[4] Faren Spark, Constance Guille and Srijan Sen, "Well-being and the risk of depression under stress", 2013.
[5] Corey L. M. Keyes, "The mental health continuum: from languishing to flourishing in life", 2002.
[6] Eric S. Kim et al., "Optimism and cause-specific mortality: A prospective cohort study", 2017.
[7] Jane Waker et al., "Major depression and survival in people with cancer", 2021.
[8] Nicholas J. L. Brown and Julia M. Rohrer, "Easy as (happiness) pie? A critical evaluation of a popular model of the determinants of well-being, 2020.
[9] https://www.hopkinsmedicine.org/health/wellness-and-prevention/risk-factors-for-heart-disease-dont-underestimate-stress
[10] https://www.who.int/news/item/02-03-2022-covid-19-pandemic-triggers-25-increase-in-prevalence-of-anxiety-and-depression-worldwide
[11] https://www.youtube.com/watch?v=7CBfCW67xT8
[12] https://www2.uwe.ac.uk/services/Marketing/students/pdf/Wellbeing-resources/well-being-scale-wemwbs.pdf

[13] https://warwick.ac.uk/fac/sci/med/research/platform/wemwbs/about/wemwbsvsswemwbs/
[14] Y. Joel Wong et al., 'Does gratitude writing improve the mental health of psychotherapy clients?" 2018.
[15] https://www.netflix.com/title/81010166

[16] https://www.hopkinsmedicine.org/health/wellness-and-prevention/forgiveness-your-health-depends-on-it
[17] A. Krusche, E. Cyhlarova and J.M.G. Williams, "Mindfulness online", 2013.
[18] Richard Chambers, Barbara Chuen Yee Lo and Nicholas B. Allen, "The impact of intensive mindfulness training on attentional control, cognitive style, and affect", 2008.

[19] Adrienne A. Taren, J. David Creswell and Peter J. Gianaros, "Dispositional mindfulness co-varies with smaller amygdala and caudate volumes in community adults", 2013.
[20] Sofie L. Valk et al., "Structural plasticity of the social brain", 2017.
[21] Tammi R. A. Kralabc et al., "Impact of short- and long-term mindfulness meditation training on amygdala reactivity to emotional stimuli", 2018.
[22] K. Otake et al., "Happy people become happier through kindness", 2006.
[23] S.D. Pressman, T.L. Kraft and M.P. Cross, "It's good to do good and receive good", 2015.
[24] S.D. Pressman, T.L., Kraft and M.P. Cross, "It's good to do good and receive good", 2015.
[25] https://fetzer.org/sites/default/files/images/stories/pdf/selfmeasures/Personality-BigFiveInventory.pdf
[26] S. Lyubomirsky, L. King and E. Diener, "The benefits of

frequent positive affect: Does happiness lead to success?" 2005.
[27] Alex Bryson and George McKerron, "Are you happy while you work?", 2017; Mappiness App, George McKerron, Susan Mouranto, London School of Economics.
[28] https://www.reuters.com/article/us-depression-risk-idUSTRE70A6TP20110111
[29] M.E.P. Seligman et al., "Explanatory style as a mechanism of disappointing athletic performance", 1990.
[30] Kube et al., "How the discrepancy between prior expectations and new information influences expectation updating in depression", 2018.
[31] Markus Zenger et al., "Pessimism predicts anxiety, depression, and quality of life in female cancer patients", 2021.
[32] Eric S. Kim et al., "Optimism and cause-specific mortality", 2017.
[33] Deborah D. Danner, David A. Snowdown and Wallace V. Friesen, "Positive emotions in early life and longevity: Findings from the nun study", 2001.
[34] E.J. Giltay et al., "Dispositional optimism and all-cause and cardiovascular mortality in a prospective cohort of elderly Dutch men and women", 2004.
[35] Suzanne C. Segerstrom, "Optimism and resources", 2007.
[36] Martin E. Seligman and Peter Schulman, "Explanatory style as a predictor of productivity and quitting among life insurance sales agents", 1986.
[37] K. K. Assad, M.B. Donnellan and R.D. Conger, "Optimism: An enduring resource for romantic relationships", 2007.
[38] S. Srivastava et al., "Optimism in close relationships",

2006.
[39] F.W. Schneider, J.A. Gruman and L.M. Coutts, *Applied Social Psychology*, 2012.
[40] G.M. Buchanan and M.E.P. Seligman, *Explanatory Style* 1995.
[41] www.authentichappiness.sas.upenn.edu/home
[42] https://www.youtube.com/watch?v=YJnZBm6Y51Y

[43] J. Kruger and D. Dunning, "Unskilled and unaware of it",1999.

[44] P. Lauster, *The Personality Test*, 1997.
[45] Pauline Walsh, Patricia Owen and Nageen Mustafa, "The creation of a confidence scale", 2021.

[46] Zachary Estes and Sydney Felker, "Confidence mediates the sex difference in mental rotation performance", 2012.
[47] https://www.psychologytoday.com/intl/blog/shyness-is-nice/201812/5-reasons-people-have-low-self-confidence.
[48] Joyce Ehrlinger and David Dunning, "How chronic self-views influence (and potentially mislead) estimates of performance", 2003.
[49] Tara Sophia Mohr, https://hbr.org/2014/08/why-women-dont-apply-for-jobs-unless-theyre-100-qualified.
[50] Linda Babcock and Sara Laschever, *Women Don't Ask: Negotiation and the Gender Divide*, 2021.
[51] Pauline Clance, Rose Imes and Suzanne Ament, "The imposter phenomenon in high achieving women", 1978.
[52] Christopher A. Pepping, Penelope J. Davis and Analise O'Donovan, "The association between state attachment security and state mindfulness", 2015.

[53] Theodore Roosevelt, https://www.commonlit.org/en/texts/the-man-in-the-arena, 1910.
[54] Lara B. Aknin, J. Kiley Hamlin and Elizabeth W. Dunn, "Giving leads to happiness in young children", 2012.
[55] L.B. Shapira and M. Mongrain, "The benefits of self-compassion and optimism exercises for individuals vulnerable to depression", 2010
[56] Emma Seppala, Timothy Rossomando and James R. Doty, "Social connection and compassion", 2013.
[57] B. J. Cosley et al. "Is compassion for others stress buffering?", 2010.
[58] L.G. Duncan, J.D. Coatsworth and M.T. Greenberg, "A model of mindful parenting", 2009.
[59] L.G. Duncan, J.D. Coatsworth and M.T. Greenberg, "A model of mindful parenting", 2009.
[60] A.B. Allen and M.R. Leary, "Self-compassion, stress, and coping", 2010.
[61] B.L. Thompson and J.A. Waltz, "Mindfulness, self-esteem, and unconditional self-acceptance", 2008.
[62] Ulli Zessin, Oliver Dickhäuser and Sven Garbade, "The relationship between self-compassion and well-being", 2015.
[63] K.D. Neff, K.L. Kirkpatrick and S.S. Rude, "Self-compassion and adaptive psychological functioning", 2007.
[64] Jason Mills and Michael Chapman, "Compassion and self-compassion in medicine," 2016.
[65] Kristin Neff, https://self-compassion.org/the-motivational-power-of-self-compassion/
[66] https://self-compassion.org/wptest/wp-content/

uploads/Self_Compassion_Scale_for_researchers.pdf

[67] https://www.cci.health.wa.gov.au/Resources/Looking-After-Yourself/Self-Compassion

[68] Dhruv Khullar, https://www.nytimes.com/2016/12/22/upshot/how-social-isolation-is-killing-us.html.

[69] https://www.adultdevelopmentstudy.org/

[70] https://newrepublic.com/article/113176/science-loneliness-how-isolation-can-kill-you

[71] Karen Bluth et al., "Does self-compassion protect adolescents from Stress?", 2015.

[72] Dale Carnegie, How to Win Friends and Influence People, 1936.

[73] Ernest L. Abel and Michael L. Kruger, "Smile intensity in photographs predicts longevity", 2010.

[74] Anthony C. Little, Benedict C. Jones and Lisa M. De Bruine, "Facial attractiveness", 2010.

[75] Gillian M. Sandstrom and Elizabeth W. Dunn, "Social interactions and well-being", 2014.

[76] https://penntoday.upenn.edu/news/social-media-use-increases-depression-and-loneliness

[77] https://www.health.harvard.edu/mind-and-mood/ramp-up-your-resilience

[78] Kate E. Murray and Alex J. Zautra, "Community resilience", 2012.

[79] Walter S. Mallory, *Edison: His Life and Inventions*, 1910.

[80] https://larryferlazzo.edublogs.org/2011/06/11/what-is-the-accurate-edison-quote-on-learning-from-failure/.

[81] Viktor Frankl, *Man's Search for Meaning*, 2004.

[82] Corey L.M. Keyes, “The mental health continuum: from languishing to flourishing in life”, 2002

ALPHABETICAL SOURCE REFERERENCES

Abel, E. L. and Kruger, M. L. (2010) "Smile intensity in photographs predicts longevity", *Psychological Science* 21(4): 542–544, https://doi.org/10.1177/0956797610363775.

Aknin, L. B., Hamlin, J. K. and Dunn, E. W. (2012) "Giving leads to happiness in young children", *PLoS One* 7(6): e39211. doi: 10.1371/journal.pone.0039211.

Allen, A. B. and Leary, M. R. (2010) "Self-compassion, stress, and coping", *Social and Personality Psychology Compass* 4(2): 107–118. https://doi.org/10.1111/j.1751-9004.2009.00246.x.

Angelou, M. (2014) "Maya Angelou: In her own words", *BBC,* 28 May, https://www.bbc.co.uk/news/world-us-canada-27610770.

Assad, K. K., Donnellan, M. B., Conger, R.D. (2007) "Optimism: An enduring resource for romantic relationships", Journal of Personality and Social Psychology 93(2): 285–297.

Babcock, L. and Laschever, S. (2021) *Women Don't Ask: Negotiation and the Gender Divide*. Princeton University Press.

Berger, M. W. (2018) "Social media use increases depression and loneliness", *Penn Today,* 9 November, https://penntoday.upenn.edu/news/social-media-use-increases-depression-and-loneliness.

Bluth, K., Roberson, P. N. E., Gaylord, S. A., Faurot, K. R.,

Grewen, K. M., Arzon, S. and Girdler, S. S. (2016) "Does self-compassion protect adolescents from stress?", Journal of Child and Family Studies 25(4): 1098–1109. doi: 10.1007/s10826-015-0307-3.

Boyd, L. (2015) "After watching this, your brain will not be the same" [online video] https://www.youtube.com/watch?v=LNHBMFCzznE.

Brief Resilience Scale (2022) https://ogg.osu.edu/media/documents/MB%20Stream/Brief%20Resilience%20Scale.pdf.

Brown, B. (2011) "The power of vulnerability" [online video] https://www.youtube.com/watch?v=iCvmsMzlF7o.

Brown, B. (2012) "Listening to shame" [online video] https://www.youtube.com/watch?v=psN1DORYYV0.

Brown, B. (2022) "Break free from shame and perfectionism" [online video] https://www.youtube.com/watch?v=MF8gTBGDMN8.

Brown, B. *The Call to Courage* [film] https://www.netflix.com/title/81010166.

Brown, N. J. L. and Rohrer, J. M. (2020) "Easy as (happiness) pie? A critical evaluation of a popular model of the determinants of well-being", *Journal of Happiness Studies* 21(4): 1285–1301.

Bryson, A. and McKerron, G. (2017) "Are you happy while you work?" The Economic Journal 127(599):

106–125.

Buchanan, G. M., & Seligman, M. E. P. (Eds.) (1995) *Explanatory Style*. Lawrence Erlbaum.

Carnegie, D. (1936) *How to Win Friends and Influence People*. Simon & Schuster.

Chambers, R., Lo, B. C. Y. and Allen, N. B. (2008) "The impact of intensive mindfulness training on attentional control, cognitive style, and affect", *Cognitive Therapy and Research* 32(3):303–322. DOI:10.1007/s10608-007-9119-0.

Clance IP Scale (2022) https://www.paulineroseclance.com/pdf/IPTestandscoring.pdf.

Clance, P., Imes, R. and Ament, S. (1978) "The imposter phenomenon in high achieving women: Dynamics and therapeutic intervention", *Psychotherapy: Theory, Research and Practice,* 15(3):241-247.

Cosley, B. J., McCoy, S. K., Saslow, L. R. and Epel, E. S. (2010) "Is compassion for others stress buffering? Consequences of compassion and social support for physiological reactivity to stress", *Journal of Experimental Social Psychology* 46(5): 816–823. https://doi.org/10.1016/j.jesp.2010.04.008.

Danner, D. D., Snowdon, D. A. and Friesen, W. V. (2001) "Positive emotions in early life and longevity: Findings from the nun study", *Journal of Personality and Social Psychology* 80(5): 804–813 https://www.apa.org/pubs/journals/releases/psp805804.pdf.

Davidson, R. J. (2019) "How mindfulness changes the emotional life of our brains" [online video] https://www.youtube.com/watch?v=7CBfCW67xT8.

Duncan, L. G., Coatsworth, J. D. and Greenberg, M. T. (2009) "A model of mindful parenting: Implications for parent–child relationships and prevention research", *Clinical Child and Family Psychology Review* 12(3): 255–270. https://doi.org/10.1007/s10567-009-0046-3.

Ehrlinger, J., and Dunning, D. (2003) "How chronic self-views influence (and potentially mislead) estimates of performance", *Journal of Personality and Social Psychology,* 84(1):5-17.

Estes, Z. and Felker, S. (2012) "Confidence mediates the sex difference in mental rotation performance", *Archives of Sexual Behavior,* 41(3):557-70.

Everett, N. (2013) "Meet yourself: A user's guide to building self-esteem" [online video] https://www.youtube.com/watch?v=uOrzmFUJtrs.

Ferlazzo. L. (2011) "What is the accurate Edison quote on learning from failure?" *Larry Ferlazzo,* 11 June, https://larryferlazzo.edublogs.org/2011/06/11/what-is-the-accurate-edison-quote-on-learning-from-failure/.

Fetzer, "The Big Five inventory" (2022) https://fetzer.org/sites/default/files/images/stories/pdf/selfmeasures/Personality-BigFiveInventory.pdf.

Frankel, V. (2004) *Man's Search for Meaning.* Rider.

Frantic World (2022) "Mindfulness, a practical guide to finding peace in a frantic world", http://www.franticworld.com.

Fredrickson, B. (2011) "The positivity ratio" [online video] https://www.youtube.com/watch?v=_hFzxfQpLjM.

Fredrickson, B. (2022) *Positivity Ratio,* http://www.positivityratio.com.

Giltay, E. J., Geleijnse, J. M., Zitman, F. G., Hoekstra, T. and Schouten, E.G. (2004) "Dispositional optimism and all-cause and cardiovascular mortality in a prospective cohort of elderly Dutch men and women", *Archives of General Psychiatry* 61(11):1126–35.

Government of Western Australia, Centre for Clinical Interventions (2022) "Self-Compassion", https://www.cci.health.wa.gov.au/Resources/Looking-After-Yourself/Self-Compassion.

Gratitude Garden App (2022) http://www.izzymcrae.com/gratitude/.

Haggerty, C. (2013) "Forgiving the unforgiveable" [online video] https://www.youtube.com/watch?v=FE7TaUG3qQI.

Harvard Medical School (2017) "Ramp up your resilience!", *Harvard Health,* 1 November, https://www.health.harvard.edu/mind-and-mood/ramp-up-your-resilience.

Harvard Study of Adult Development (2022), https://www.adultdevelopmentstudy.org/.

Johns Hopkins Medicine (2022) "Forgiveness: Your health depends on it", https://www.hopkinsmedicine.org/health/wellness-and-prevention/forgiveness-your-health-depends-on-it.

Johns Hopkins Medicine (2022) "Risk factors for heart disease: Please don't underestimate stress", https://www.hopkinsmedicine.org/health/wellness-and-prevention/risk-factors-for-heart-disease-dont-underestimate-stress.

Keltner, D. (2014) "We are built to be kind" [online video] https://www.youtube.com/watch?v=SsWs6bf7tvI.

Keyes C. L. M. (2002) "The mental health continuum: From languishing to flourishing in life", *Journal of Health and Social Research* 43 (June): 207–222.

Khullar, D. (2016) "How social isolation is killing us", *New York Times,* 22 December, https://www.nytimes.com/2016/12/22/upshot/how-social-isolation-is-killing-us.html.

Kim, E. S., Hagan, K. A., Grodstein, F., DeMeo, D. L., De

Vivo, I. and Kubzansky, L. D. (2017) "Optimism and cause-specific mortality: A prospective cohort study", *American Journal of Epidemiology* 185(1): 21–29.

Kralabc, T. R. A., Schuyler, B. S., Mumfordac, J. A., Rosenkranz, M., Lutz Ace, A. and Davidson, R. J. (2018) "Impact of short- and long-term mindfulness meditation training on amygdala reactivity to emotional stimuli", *Neuroimage* 181:301–313.

Kruger, J. and Dunning, D. (1999) "Unskilled and unaware of it: How difficulties in recognising one's own incompetence leads to inflated self-assessments", Journal of Personality and Social Psychology 77(6): 1121–34 DOI:10.1037//0022-3514.77.6.1121.

Krusche, A., Cyhlarova, E. and Williams, J. M. G. (2013) "Mindfulness online: An evaluation of the feasibility of a web-based mindfulness course for stress, anxiety and depression", *BMJ Open* 3: e003498. doi: 10.1136/bmjopen-2013-003498.

Kube, T., Kirchner, L., Lemmer, G. and Glombiewski, J. A. (2021) How the discrepancy between prior expectations and new information influences expectation updating in depression: The greater, the better?", *Clinical Psychological Science* 10(3): 430–449.

Lauster, P. (1997) *The Personality Test.* Pan Books.

Lewis Psychology (2021) "ABCDE model: Challenge the pessimistic thoughts" [online video] https://

www.youtube.com/watch?v=YJnZBm6Y51Y.

Little, A. C., Jones, B. C. and De Bruine, L. M. (2010) "Facial attractiveness: Evolutionary based research", Philosophical Transactions of The Royal Society B Biological Sciences 366(1571): 1638–59, DOI:10.1098/rstb.2010.0404.

Luskin, F. (2012) "The science of happiness" [online video] https://www.youtube.com/watch?v=Qvfauh-XZiQ.

Lyubomirsky, S., King, L. and Diener, E. (2005) "The benefits of frequent positive affect: Does happiness lead to success?" *Psychological Bulletin American Psychological Association* 131(6): 803– 855.

Mallory, W. S. (1910) *Edison: His Life and Inventions.* Harper & Brothers.

Mappiness App [application], dev. George McKerron and Susan Mouranto, London School of Economics. http://www.mappiness.org.uk/.

Markaway, B. (2018) "5 reasons people have low self-confidence", *Psychology today,* 7 December, https://www.psychologytoday.com/intl/blog/shyness-is-nice/201812/5-reasons-people-have-low-self-confidence.

Markaway, B. and Ampel, C. (2018) *The Self-Confidence Workbook: A Guide to Overcoming Self-Doubt and Improving Self-Esteem.* Althea Press.

Mills, J. and Chapman, M. (2016) "Compassion and self-compassion in medicine: Self-care for the caregiver", *The Australasian Medical Journal* 9(5): 87–91.

MindToolsVideos (2014) "How to recognise and cure perfectionism" [online video] https://www.youtube.com/watch?v=zTj25XawoDk.

Mohr, T. S. (2014) "Why women don't apply for jobs unless they're 100% qualified", *Harvard Business Review,* 26 August, https://hbr.org/2014/08/why-women-dont-apply-for-jobs-unless-theyre-100-qualified.

Murray, K. E. and Zautra, A. J. (2012) "Community resilience: Fostering recovery, sustainability, and growth", in M. Ungar (Ed.), *The Social Ecology of Resilience: A Handbook of Theory and* Practice (pp. 337–345), Springer Science. DOI:10.1007/978-1-4614-0586-3_26.

Neff, K. (2022) "The motivational power of self-compassion", https://self-compassion.org/the-motivational-power-of-self-compassion/.

Neff, K. (2022) "The three components of self-compassion", https://self-compassion.org/the-three-elements-of-self-compassion-2/.

Neff, K. D., Kirkpatrick, K. L. and Rude, S. S. (2007) "Self-compassion and adaptive psychological functioning", *Journal of Research in Personality* 41(1):

139–154. https://doi.org/10.1016/j.jrp.2006.03.004.

Norton, A. (2011) "Optimistic teens show lower depression risk", *Reuters,* 11 January, https://www.reuters.com/article/us-depression-risk-idUSTRE70A6TP20110111.

Optimism Test [online], University of Pennsylvania https://www.authentichappiness.sas.upenn.edu/testcenter.

Otake, K., Shimai, S., Tanaka-Matsumi, J., Otsui, K. and Fredrickson, B. L. (2006), "Happy people become happier through kindness: A counting kindnesses intervention", *Journal of Happiness Studies* 7(3):361–75.

Participant (2013) "Why happy people do it better: The science of happiness" [online video] https://www.youtube.com/watch?v=IkMHZ7mchVo.

Pepping, C. A., Davis, P. J. and O'Donovan, A. (2015) "The association between state attachment security and state mindfulness", *PLoS ONE* 10(3): e0116779 https://doi.org/10.1371/journal.pone.0116779.

Pinker, S. (2017) "The secret to living longer may be your social life" [online video] https://www.youtube.com/watch?v=ptIecdCZ3dg.

Pressman, S. D., Kraft, T. L. and Cross, M. P. (2015) "It's good to do good and receive good: The impact of a 'pay it forward' style kindness intervention on giver and receiver well-being", *Journal of Positive Psychology*

10(4):293–302.

Race, K. (2015) "Generation stress: From surviving to thriving" [online video] https://www.youtube.com/watch?v=7jRND5IU3Qg.

Reiss, H. (2013) "The power of empathy" [online video] https://www.youtube.com/watch?v=baHrcC8B4WM.

Remes, O. (2018) "How to get rid of loneliness and become happy" [online video] https://www.youtube.com/watch?v=vZT-bB66iIk.

Roosevelt, T. (1910) "Citizenship in a republic", delivered Sorbonne Paris, 23rd April 1910, https://www.commonlit.org/en/texts/the-man-in-the-arena.

Rose, R. (2019) "From stress to resilience" [online video] https://www.youtube.com/watch?v=Q7vYuKvpneM.

Rosenberg Self-Esteem Scale (2022) https://wwnorton.com/college/psych/psychsci/media/rosenberg.htm.

Salzberg, S. (2015) "Where does compassion really come from?" [online video] https://www.youtube.com/watch?v=A4a66aFaIME.

Sandstrom, G. M. and Dunn, E. W. (2014) "Social interactions and well-being: The surprising power of weak ties", Personality and Social Psychology Bulletin

40(7): 910–922, doi: 10.1177/0146167214529799.

Schneider, F. W., Gruman, J. A., & Coutts, L. M. (2012) *Applied Social Psychology: Understanding and Addressing Social and Practical Problems* (2nd ed.). Sage Publications.

Science Insider (2018) "What having a dog does to your brain" [online video] https://www.youtube.com/watch?v=w0K6UBzGQ7E.

Segerstrom, S. C. (2007) "Optimism and resources: Effects on each other and on health over 10 years", *Journal of Research in Personality* 41(4):10.1016/j.jrp.2006.09.004. doi: 10.1016/j.jrp.2006.09.004.

Self-Compassion Scale (2022) https://self-compassion.org/wptest/wp-content/uploads/Self_Compassion_Scale_for_researchers.pdf.

Seligman, M. (2006) *Learned Optimism: How to Change Your Mind and Your Life.* Vintage.

Seligman, M. (2009) "Dr. Seligman's definition of optimism" [online video] https://www.youtube.com/watch?v=8-rMuJW-UKg.

Seligman, M. E. and Schulman, P. (1986) "Explanatory style as a predictor of productivity and quitting among life insurance sales agents", *Journal of Personality and Social Psychology*, 50(4): 832–838. https://doi.org/10.1037/0022-3514.50.4.832.

Seligman, M. E. P., Nolen-Hoeksema, S., Thornton, N.

and Thornton, K. M. (1990) "Explanatory style as a mechanism of disappointing athletic performance", Psychological Science 1(2): 143–146.

Seppala, E., Rossomando, T. and Doty, J. R. (2013) "Social connection and compassion: Important predictors of health and well-being", *Journal of Social Research* 80(2): 411–430.

Shapira, L. B. and Mongrain, M. (2010) "The benefits of self-compassion and optimism exercises for individuals vulnerable to depression", *The Journal of Positive Psychology*, 5(5), 377–389. https://doi.org/10.1080/17439760.2010.516763.

Sharot, T. (2012) "The optimism bias" [online video] https://www.youtube.com/watch?v=B8rmi95pYL0.

Sharot, T. (2014) "How to motivate yourself to change your behaviour" [online video] https://www.youtube.com/watch?v=xp0O2vi8DX4.

Shulevitz, J. (2013) "The lethality of loneliness: We now know it can ravage our body and brain", *The New Republic,* 13 May, https://newrepublic.com/article/113176/science-loneliness-how-isolation-can-kill-you.

Sinek, S. (2020) "How I became an optimist" [online video] https://www.youtube.com/watch?v=lcja1Hi39aQ.

Solomon, L. (2016) "The surprising solution to the imposter syndrome" [online video] https://

www.youtube.com/watch?v=whyUPLJZljE.

Spark, F., Guille, C. and Sen, S. (2013) "Well-being and the risk of depression under stress", *PLoS One* 8(7): e67395.

Srivastava, S., McGonigal, K. M., Richards, J. M., Butler, E. A. and Gross, J. J. (2006) "Optimism in close relationships: How seeing things in a positive light makes them so", Journal of Personality and Social Psychology 91(1): 143–153.

Taren, A. A., Creswell, J. D. and Gianaros, P. J. (2013) "Dispositional mindfulness co-varies with smaller amygdala and caudate volumes in community adults", *PLoS One* 8(5): e64574. doi: 10.1371/journal.pone.0064574.

The Almost Perfect Scale (2020) https://heartofsubstance.com/wp-content/uploads/2020/02/Almost-Perfect-Scale_updatedversion.pdf.

Thompson, B. L. and Waltz, J. A. (2008) "Mindfulness, self-esteem, and unconditional self-acceptance", *Journal of Rational-Emotive & Cognitive-Behavior Therapy* 26(2): 119–126. https://doi.org/10.1007/s10942-007-0059-0.

Twill (2015) "Why mindfulness is a superpower" [online video] https://www.youtube.com/watch?v=w6T02g5hnT4.

Tyrrel, M. (2019) "Treating perfectionism: 3 therapy

strategies" [online video] https://www.youtube.com/watch?v=T1bg7I2bXBU.

Urban, T. (2016) "Inside the mind of the master procrastinator" [online video] https://www.youtube.com/watch?v=arj7oStGLkU.

Valk, S. L., Bernhardt, B. C., Trautwein, F.-M., Böckler, A., Kanske, P., Guizard, N., Collins, D. L. and Singer, T. (2017) "Structural plasticity of the social brain: Differential change after socio-affective and cognitive mental training", *Science Advances* 3(10): e1700489.

Waldinger, R. (2016) "What makes a good life? Lessons from the longest study on happiness" [online video] https://www.youtube.com/watch?v=8KkKuTCFvzI.

Walker, J., Mulick, A., Magill, N., Symeonides, ... et al. (2021) "Major depression and survival in people with cancer", *Psychosomatic Medicine* 83(5): 410–416.

Walsh, P., Owen, P. and Mustafa, N. (2021) "The creation of a confidence scale: The confidence in managing challenging situations scale", *Journal of Research in Nursing* 26(6): 1–14.

Warwick University (2022) *The Warwick-Edinburgh Mental Wellbeing Scale* https://warwick.ac.uk/fac/sci/med/research/platform/wemwbs/about/wemwbsvsswemwbs/.

Warwick-Edinburgh Mental Wellbeing Scale (2022) https://www2.uwe.ac.uk/services/Marketing/

students/pdf/Wellbeing-resources/well-being-scale-wemwbs.pdf.

Watkins, A. (2012) "Being brilliant every single day (Part 1 and 2)" [online videos] https://www.youtube.com/watch?v=q06YIWCR2Js, https://www.youtube.com/watch?v=Q_fFattg8N0.

Westerhof, G. J. and Keyes, C. L. M. (2010) "Mental illness and mental health: The two continua model across the lifespan", *Journal of Adult Development* 17(2): 110–119.

Williams, M. (2011) "The science of mindfulness" [online video] https://www.youtube.com/watch?v=8GVwnxkWmSM.

Wong, Y. J., Owen, J., Gabana, N. T., Brown, J. W., McInnis, S., Toth, P. and Gilman, L. (2016) "Does gratitude writing improve the mental health of psychotherapy clients? Evidence from a randomized controlled trial", *Psychotherapy Research* 28(2): 192–202.

World Health Organization, "Covid-19 pandemic triggers 25% increase in prevalence of anxiety and depression worldwide", https://www.who.int/news/item/02-03-2022-covid-19-pandemic-triggers-25-increase-in-prevalence-of-anxiety-and-depression-worldwide.

Zenger, M., Gleasner, H., Höckel, M. and Hinz, A. (2011) "Pessimism predicts anxiety, depression, and quality of life in female cancer patients", *Japanese Journal of Clinical Oncology* 41(1):87–94. doi: 10.1093/jjco/hyq168.

Zessin, U., Dickhäuser, O. and Garbade, S. (2015) "The relationship between self-compassion and well-being: A meta-analysis", Applied Psychological Health and Well Being 7(3):340–64. doi: 10.1111/aphw.12051.

Printed in Great Britain
by Amazon

26173930R00148